DATE		

DISCARD

® THE BAKER & TAYLOR CO.

KNOXVILLE TENNESSEE

Knoxville, Tennessee

CONTINUITY AND CHANGE
IN AN APPALACHIAN CITY

Michael J. McDonald and
William Bruce Wheeler

THE UNIVERSITY OF TENNESSEE PRESS ★ KNOXVILLE

Library of Congress Cataloging in Publication Data

McDonald, Michael J., 1934-
  Knoxville, Tennessee: continuity and change in an Appalachian city.

  Bibliography: p.
  Includes index.
  1. Knoxville (Tenn.)—Economic conditions. 2. Knoxville (Tenn.)—Social
conditions. 3. Knoxville (Tenn.)—Politics and government. 4. Knoxville (Tenn.)—
History. I. Wheeler, William Bruce, 1939–   .
II. Title
HC108.K6M33   1983   330.9768'85   83-1402
ISBN 0-87049-393-0

CONTENTS ★

MAPS ★

TABLES ★

ILLUSTRATIONS ★

KNOXVILLE, TENNESSEE

IN DECEMBER 1978 *The South Magazine*, a publication devoted to southern business leaders, featured an article on Knoxville, Tennessee, that attempted to capture the spirit of the city's past, present, and future. Significantly, it began, "Rip Van Winkle would be at home in Knoxville these days. For the past 20 years, while other cities of the South sprang awake with economic activity, Knoxville held steadfastly to its traditionally ultraconservative ways. Now, with suddenness, it is astir with economic excitement few southern cities, not even Atlanta, have experienced at one gush." Although the article made almost no stir in the Knoxville community itself, its principal message—that Knoxville, after years of being virtually undisturbed by change, was on the brink of changes so important and profound that the city would be radically different in the near future—had long been sensed by Knoxvillians. Indeed, whether they yearned for change or opposed it as vociferously as their East Tennessee forebears had battled Satan and modernization, most knew or felt the ambivalent promise of transformation.

At the same time that Knoxvillians sensed the winds of change, another series of apparently unrelated events was taking place. After a period of almost uninterrupted neglect, Knoxvillians were beginning to show an interest that approached fascination with the city's past. Their aroused concern with Knoxville's history took many forms. In 1976 *Heart of the Valley*, published by the East Tennessee Historical Society, provided a much-needed update of Mary U. Rothrock's *The French Broad–Holston Country* (1946). Judith Clayton Isenhour's well-received *Knoxville: A Pictorial History* (1978) offered a delightful look at the city's past. In 1975 an ambitious project was undertaken to set up a combined city-county historical and archival collection, eventually to be merged with the McClung Historical Collection in the renovated Customs House. Interest in historical preservation and restoration reached an all-time high. And finally, educational institutions, from county schools to the University of Tennessee, offered students opportunities to explore the historical byways of the East Tennessee city. In short, Knoxville appeared to have become enamored with the study of its own past.

These two trends, the pervasive sense of change and the fascination with the city's history, were not unrelated. Quite the opposite. As Knoxvillians came to believe that their city stood on the brink of almost fathomless change, they similarly sensed that their past was in danger of being lost, forgotten, or bulldozed into obscurity. Their reaction was like that of other communities with similar experiences, promises, and fears. In the eyes of many, as unpleasant as some aspects of Knoxville's past had been, that past would surely be more comfortable than an uncertain future.

The authors join fellow Knoxvillians in seeking an understanding of the city's past, not by confronting historically all of the tangible aspects of that past, but selecting some of them so as to provide a working hypothesis, a guide to aid us in assessing where we are and what we are as a city.

The authors therefore have eschewed much of the city's earlier history, preferring to begin with Knoxville's transformation from a commercial to an industrial center. This transformation gained momentum in the late nineteenth and early twentieth century, at precisely the time when southern Appalachian birthrates were beginning to create serious pressures on the marginal and eroded lands of the region's subsistence farmers and when the earlier black freedmen's migrations to Knoxville were swelled by a general black exodus from the rural South. The conjuncture of industrial growth and rural-to-urban migration, especially that from Appalachia, marks the beginning of a period when the city fulfills a functional role long familiar to students of modernization—the ability to absorb labor from a rural hinter-land. This absorptive role is a helpful one in understanding the beginnings of the industrial revolution in Britain. Why should it be applied to the subject of this book?

Urban absorption of hinterland labor is one of the characteristics inherent in the transformation of premodern to modern societies in western Europe and Britain in the nineteenth century. It is applicable to Knoxville because industrial Knoxville absorbed, even in the late nineteenth and early twen-tieth century, Appalachian and southern black labor, both of which groups came from what could be termed "premodern" environments, or at least "transitional" ones between premodern and modern.

Henry Shapiro, in his excellent book *Appalachia on Our Mind*, has argued that the "otherness" and strangeness of Appalachia is an intellectual artifact produced in part by America's unwillingness to recognize plurality in our society and instead to treat Appalachia as an entity, a population, and a culture that must become modernized—a last anomaly in our progressive vision of America.[1] There is much truth in Shapiro's thesis, but the region's character rests on more than an intellectual perception of Appalachia. It

---

[1] Henry Shapiro, *Appalachia On Our Mind: The Southern Mountains and Mountaineers in The American Consciousness, 1870–1920* (Chapel Hill, 1978).

rests on the observed and measured reality of the effects of isolation, poor transportation, lack of economic mobility, limited education, and often, economic deprivation. These qualities, which modernization strives to alleviate, are joined by other Appalachian qualities like self-reliance, community cohesiveness, kin and networks of aid and help, and a host of virtues often tagged simply as "rural."

In truth, many qualities that we call "Appalachian" are, rather, characteristics of rural areas that are characterized by subsistence farming or farming mixed with the extractive industries like (in the 1910s and 1920s of the twentieth century) logging and, later, mining. But they are characteristics of what might be termed economic deviation, or "otherness," from mainstream America. We have used the term "Appalachia" and "Appalachian" to denote generally an environment that is premodern or transitional—an environment of rurality, strong kinship ties, community, low social mobility, resistance to change, self-awareness, and deep personal religious conviction.

No one would argue that one has to live in Appalachia to possess these characteristics. One can simply assert that these characteristics in Appalachia exist in a concentrated and self-conscious mode that is increasingly at variance with the characteristics of urban America in the late nineteenth and in the twentieth century. The phrase "at variance" is intended to signify that a feeling of "otherness" exists between urban American and Appalachian values—not the real or imagined superiority of one over the other.

One is tempted simply to use Knoxville as a model (in an urban historical sense) for all small and mid-sized U.S. cities, and, superficially, this can be done. But because the values, characteristics, and "otherness" of Appalachia inhere in Knoxville, in an urban setting, and take on or impart to Knoxville an Appalachian style and tone that is culturally and politically different in many respects from other areas, Knoxville seems inappropriate as a generalized American model.

Granted, at some time or other, all southern cities have been peopled by rural persons who carried to urban centers rural culture and social elements. Why should Knoxville be different? The difference, we feel, lies in the rate and degree of absorption of Appalachia by the New South industrial city. Knoxville is not like Atlanta. It has attracted rural Appalachia, but its industrial and economic base has experienced neither steady nor constant growth and as a result its "urbanness" has not been dynamic enough to leach out Appalachian characteristics and transform its citizens into simply southern urbanites. Knoxville's location, too, has kept its inhabitants in almost constant touch with Appalachian values—the rural hinterland has been, and in some cases still is, symbiotically and symbolically linked to Knoxville in a much deeper and constant sense than is the case with most southern cities.

An urban history which uses the concepts "New South" and "Appalachia" promises at the very least to be conflict-ridden, for no two terms are crowded with more dissonant images than these two. Henry Grady envisioned a New South of cities, factories and mills, which were intended to stop the hemorrhage of youth and talent out of the South and create an industrial base that would eventually raise the standard of living and create a quality of life commensurate with that enjoyed by the rest of the nation. Ultimately, Grady's vision was challenged by the Vanderbilt University "fugitives," who responded to industrial growth by lauding the rural South and its virtuous love of the soil, of kin and neighbor, and of the rural life and its values against the industrial devaluation of life and the environment.

These polar positions on rural life, urbanization and modernity are perhaps couched in different terms today, but the basic argument is little changed. The proponents of the New South have always urged industrial development and in fact still do. Their opponents, these days, often evoke "Appalachia" in defense of real or imagined rural virtues and culture, placing it as a keyword in the forefront of an attack upon the despoilment of an ecologically fragile environment.

The debate over modernization, urbanization and rural culture in the South is an old one, and an ongoing one. What the polar positions disguise, however, is the inherent ambiguity represented in both the New South and Appalachia, an ambiguity well illustrated by Benjamin Disraeli's novel *Coningsby*. Coningsby laments to his friend Sidonia: "What I would not give to see Athens!" Sidonia contemptuously replies, "Phantoms and spectres! The age of ruins is past. Have you seen Manchester ?"

Southerners, urban and rural, since the Civil War have been tantalized by their visions of Athens and Manchester. Cities of the "age of ruins," cities of the mind, have been the special preserve of those who battle encroaching modernity and Henry Grady's New South Manchesters. But truly, the promotion of and the opposition to growth, development, and industrialization have been only contrapuntal streams of a Greek chorus alternately in support of or opposed to modernization. But the real question is not whether modernization and urbanization is good—for these have been dominant forces in twentieth-century American life—but rather what constitutes the good city.

The authors see the good city as a community founded on responsible growth, on development that can accommodate an indigenous culture, and on industrialism that can provide jobs and a rising standard of living without accompanying environmental and human degradation. Grady had seen industrial growth as the stimulus that would regenerate the South financially, economically, and socially. He saw jobs, capital formation, and growth as panaceas for the problems of the South's hard-pressed agricultural base. How well Grady and other early proponents of the New South understood the ambivalence of modernization, which would cause Alexis de Tocqueville to say of Manchester that "From this filthy sewer pure gold flows," is open to question. To join the issue fully, it is only fair to state that the authors embrace neither extremes of the argument, for Appalachia and against the New South, nor vice versa. We are ambiguists—historians assessing the city's tortuous path along the lines of its development. Granted, concerns about growth and development have loomed large in this history, but only because the stages of Knoxville's transition have been posited on demographic and economic issues and the political structures attached to them rather than on any insistence that change itself is inherently good.

If the history of Knoxville is the story of the New South's coming to Appalachia, it is fair to say that it is also the story of Appalachia's coming to the New South. This notion burdens the reader with more imagery than any author has the right to create, but since there are two of us perhaps it is permissible. At any rate, the industrial base of the New South did come to Knoxville, which is in the midst of the southern Appalachians, and because it did, Appalachian people came to Knoxville.

The relationship of Appalachia and the New South was, in the beginning, a purely symbiotic arrangement in Knoxville. Industrial growth provided the jobs that allowed many people from Appalachia to escape what, in many instances, were unproductive subsistence farms or sharecroppers' plots. This symbiotic relationship is important to our story for a number of reasons: the first generation of industrial workers who came to fill the industrial jobs of the New South from the hills and hollows of Appalachia or the agricultural communities of the Old South came because the industrial jobs held the promise of improvement. But they had to endure the most difficult of adjustments to industrial life. Consciously or unconsciously, they had to adjust their cultural values to an industrial structure, or frame them out to fit in an urban environment. The result, we feel, was the style of the Appalachian New South—industry and industrial growth amidst an atmosphere of cultural conservatism, a conservatism designed to provide roots and nurture in an urban environment that was in many, if not in most respects, alien to both the white and the black mill hands who were drawn to the city. After all, the eminent black sociologist from Fisk, Charles Johnson, had warned blacks, after visiting the cities of Tennessee in the 1930s, of the corrosive character of urbanism and industrialism on the black community and its values. Blacks and Appalachian whites alike sensed the deep ambiguity in the urban industrial existence—the constantly alternating threat and promise of modernization—and they adjusted their cultural mores and politics to allow Appalachian and black culture to bloom in an urban environment. This remains the key to what has puzzled many visitors to Knoxville—its combination of rural attitudes with the economic infrastructure of an industrial city. The two seemed out of sync with one another, almost as though rural southern and Appalachian ways were unassimilable in the alien environment of modern urbanism.

If, however, the conservativism of the city's labor force had explicable origins, that of the city's economic and social elites was less so. The commercial barons of the city's immediate postwar development gave way, in time, to an infusion of mill owners and industrialists who in turn eventually had to make way for the developers. Groups that had at one point constituted the cutting edge of change fell back on conservativism and often on political lassitude. Hence, what could be termed the civic-commercial elite of the city was constantly changing, both in composition and attitude. The conservatism of the city's older elites and that of its laborers stamped Knoxville, to many, as a dreary little mill town, and there were many in these two groups who liked it that way, preferring constancy and the familiar over change in any form. The culture of mill hand and mill owner then made a rather odd but effective political block to change, but within Knoxville, and from outside the area, there had constantly been growing a third and much less conservative "culture," a culture which—for good or ill—was preoccupied with development, economic growth, and progress. This third culture was rooted among the native Knoxvillians and East Tennesseans who had, in effect, "made good" by moving up the social ladder. In the early 1980s Knoxville's Mayor Randy Tyree and banker and ex-gubernatorial candidate Jake Butcher are but the most visible of these, along with former mayor Kyle Testerman. They and their ilk were joined by the influx of potential proponents of development from the Tennessee Valley Authority (TVA), the University of Tennessee, and Oak Ridge. Many of these became the supporters and boosters of industrial site development, downtown development and revitalization, metropolitan government, and, finally, Expo '82 and the World's Fair concept. The native growth-oriented boosters found that the demographic and economic currents of the 1950s and 1960s moved to further their designs. Industrial retardation in Knoxville coupled with spreading industrial locations on a regional basis helped to make the city increasingly oriented toward service and government (federal and municipal), which in turn attracted newcomers from outside and caused many industrial workers to seek employment elsewhere. For the development mentality, the conjuncture of an influx of the upwardly mobile with a hemorrhage outward of the temporarily immobile was favorable. It balanced the development-progressive forces against the elite and Appalachian conservatives in favor of the developers, setting Knoxville on a new path.

For much of its history, Knoxville's conservative elites had left politics to the representatives of the Appalachian and black poor because they were as recognizably unthreatening most of the time; they, too, resisted change. The coalition of newcomers and native boosters broke what they saw as an unpleasant and unwarrantable deadlock and set about changing the city's image. For good or ill, the city is, at least temporarily, on that path.

The purpose of this book is a simple one. As more and more newcomers move to the Knoxville area and as an increasing number of older Knoxvillians begin to probe their collective past, certain questions are asked repeatedly. "Why is Knoxville the way it is?" "What does it mean to be a Knoxvillian?" "How can anyone understand Knoxville?" This book is an extended historical essay that seeks less to answer these questions (for no history could answer them definitively) than to provide an analytical framework within which Knoxvillians and other urban southerners can examine these questions in the light of their own experiences. Cities have passed through a succession of crises since World War II, owing largely to fluctuations in population and economic movements and their results. As a consequence, urban people, north and south, east and west, have become more concerned with how they came to be where and what they are. In that way, Knoxville and Knoxvillians are no different from urbanites everywhere.

CHAPTER ONE ★ *The New South Comes to Appalachia:*
The Emergence of Industrial Knoxville,
1865–1940

YEARS AFTER the Civil War, Atlanta editor and sectional booster Henry Grady celebrated what he chose to call the "New South," a South that had risen out of the ashes of defeat to embrace the modern industrial age with a fervor usually confined to religious crusades. Although Grady and his New South cohorts often confused what they hoped for with what was actually accomplished, it is clear that in the years immediately following the Civil War a new spirit manifested itself in most of the states of the former Confederacy, a spirit that discarded older notions of an agricultural South and turned instead to industrialization, urbanization, and economic diversification. In a characteristic New South address to the New England Society of New York in 1886, Grady unveiled his section to a delighted audience.

> But what is the sum of our work? We have found out that in the summing up the free negro counts more than he did as a slave. . . . We have sown towns and cities in the place of theories, and put business above politics . . . and have . . . wiped out the place where Mason and Dixon's line used to be.
> Never was nobler duty confided to human hands than the uplifting and upbuilding of the prostrate and bleeding South—misguided, perhaps, but beautiful in her suffering. . . . In the record of her social, industrial, and political illustration we await with confidence the verdict of the world.[1]

Knoxville, Tennessee, was very much a part of the New South movement. At the outset of the Civil War, Knoxville was a modest town that had served successively as a speculative venture, a seat of government, a way-station through which travelers heading west would pass, a small commercial center, and (by the time of the Civil War) one of several towns on the

---

[1] For stimulating treatments of the myth and reality of the New South see C. Vann Woodward, *Origins of the New South, 1877–1914*, vol. IX in Wendell Holmes Stephenson and E. Merton Coulter, eds., *A History of the South* (Baton Rouge, 1951), and Paul M. Gaston, *The New South Creed: A Study in Southern Mythmaking* (New York, 1970). For Grady's address see Henry Grady, "The New South," in Richard N. Current and John A. Garraty, eds., *Words that Made American History* (Boston, 1962), II, 24–31.

railroad lines that linked the South to the more dynamic regions to the north and west.[2]

But the romantic and ambitious New South idea had infected a portion of the town's close-knit civic-commercial elite, men whose interests in banking, railroads, expanded wholesaling and retailing capacities, and real estate development made them ideal converts to the New South creed. For these men the great dream was that the fortuitous combination of natural resources, outside capital, good rail connections, and the heretofore virtually untapped labor pool of the surrounding hinterland would make of Knoxville a major commercial and industrial center. After all, wasn't Big Lick soon to become Roanoke? Wasn't Atlanta once Terminus, Georgia?[3]

And by the advent of World War II it appeared that those grandiose dreams had come true. The city had become, in successive turns, a major wholesaling and manufacturing center, and population growth from 1865 to 1940 had been truly impressive. Yet the New South exacted a high price, both from those who embraced it and from those caught in the wheels of change. Rural whites and blacks who moved from the agriculturally overpopulated hinterland in search of employment soon learned that industrialization and urban life threatened to cut them off from the traditional culture and institutions they valued so highly. They strongly resisted the threats. Bankers and businessmen who had been the original architects of the New South credo also found themselves resisting some changes; the depressions of the 1890s and the 1930s and what they saw as the political excesses of those who spoke for the working-class whites and blacks caused them either to abandon the city, withdraw from the savage political arena, or alter the city's political institutions so as to give them more power to fulfill their vision. As the city grew, it lost what sense of unity it previously had possessed, dividing into mutually suspicious socioeconomic and political camps that sporadically attacked one another but were not powerful enough to control or direct Knoxville's economic growth. Knoxville entered the modern urban age ambivalent and divided, apparently either unwilling or unable to alter its physical or spiritual environment. Urbanization had come to Appalachia, but the New South dream had its darker side.

KNOXVILLE IN PEACE AND WAR

For both good and ill, Knoxville's early history had been intimately linked to the economic, political, demographic, and social history of East Tennes-

[2]For a good portrait of Knoxville before the Civil War see Mary U. Rothrock, ed., *The French Broad–Holston Country: A History of Knox County, Tennessee* (Knoxville, 1946), 34–123.

[3]Woodward, *Origins of the New South*, 124, 142–74.

see. The mountains that residents and tourists alike now admire were initially great barriers preventing the region's significant population growth in the antebellum years. Moreover, the area's climate and terrain seem to have made it inhospitable for the rise of large plantations and of slavery. Those men and women who did arrive in Knoxville prior to the Civil War usually were but travelers searching for better land and opportunities westward. Knoxville earned a reputation as a comparatively wild town, boasting of (or embarrassed by) an abundance of taverns and tippling houses (far outnumbering churches), gambling and prostitution, riverboat men, and the seemingly endless trickle of passers-through. Efforts by the town's citizens in the 1830s to wipe out liquor sales and prostitution were quixotic and generally unsuccessful.

Economics, cultural characteristics of the population, and physical isolation led the East Tennessee region into different political paths than those of the western and middle parts of the state, creating an intrastate political rivalry that has not disappeared. Like the mountain areas of Virginia and North Carolina, East Tennesee fought running political battles with other regions of the state over legislative appointments, taxation, internal improvements, slavery, and, finally, whether Tennessee should join other southern states in secession. Such conflicts helped to create the stereotype of East Tennesseans as a provincial and suspicious lot, wary of government (which many were convinced was corrupt and conducted solely for the benefit of someone else), lawless, fiercely loyal to kin and clan, and wary of all outsiders, a stereotype that was less false than overdrawn.[4]

Knoxville's ruling class in the prewar years was homogeneous. Composed mostly of merchants, professional men, and large real estate holders descended from some of the town's original settlers (when Knoxville, prior to 1792, was known as White's Fort), this elite group was growing progressively wealthier as secession approached. A large proportion were Presbyterians, most belonging to the socially acceptable First Presbyterian Church. A majority owned few if any slaves, mostly house servants.[5]

As early as the 1830s Knoxville's elite group recognized the benefits rail connections would bring both to the town and to themselves. Endless meetings, subscriptions of private monies, and even voting of public funds (once even taking $50,000 supposedly set aside for a new waterworks) brought extremely slow results, due largely to difficult topography and shaky financial backing of the proposed lines. By the Civil War, however, Knoxville

[4]For a good discussion of East Tennessee prior to the Civil War see Charles Faulkner Bryan, Jr., "The Civil War in East Tennessee: A Social, Political, and Economic Study" (Ph.D. diss., Univ. of Tennessee, 1978), ch. 1. See also Stanley J. Folmsbee, Robert E. Corlew, and Enoch L. Mitchell, *Tennessee, A Short History* (Knoxville, 1969), 163–66.

[5]On Knoxville's elite see Karen Thornton, "The Elite of Knoxville: Tennessee in the Age of Jackson" (unpub. paper in possession of the author).

had full rail connections as far as New York City, although economic ties with Virginia and other southern states via those rail connections clearly marked the town's commercial economy as southern-oriented. Indeed, largely for that reason most of Knoxville's merchants, bankers, professional men, and large real estate holders would support the Confederacy while the region all around them displayed marked anti-Confederate sentiments. So strong was the pro-Confederate feeling among the Knoxville elite that the First Presbyterian Church (where most of them worshipped) was taken over by the Union Army when it occupied Knoxville in 1863 and was not returned to the church's elders until a year after the war ended.[6]

Ostensibly, Knoxville's city government was democratic, at least after 1839 when the mayoralty became an elective office. But for all practical purposes the town's elite continued to preside over local affairs almost unchallenged. In 1860 fewer than a third of the eligible voters cast ballots in that year's mayoralty race, and other election statistics (with the exception of the ballots on the question of secession) reinforce the impression that most Knoxvillians deferred to the town's mercantile and professional nabobs. Simultaneously it appears that the citizens simply ignored ordinances and regulations that they felt impinged on their individual rights or personal liberty. Hence, one can say that Knoxville's elite had great power and at the same time was essentially powerless.[7]

Though rail linkages had done little by the Civil War to benefit the town economically, those same linkages made Knoxville a strategic objective of no little importance. For the Confederacy, the railroad was vital for moving men and supplies to the Virginia theater. For the Union, the capture of Knoxville would break the rebels' supply lines, serve as a wedge for future offensives into the heart of the Confederacy, and provide an uplift in morale for East Tennessee Unionists (an important consideration in the eyes of President Lincoln). Thus, in 1863, when the Confederacy suffered the dual defeats at Gettysburg and Vicksburg (losing over 28,000 at Gettysburg and an additional 40,000 at Vicksburg), the Union Army in Tennessee felt free to move eastward from Nashville to brush Bragg away and take Knoxville. Indeed, Knoxville, once having sworn allegiance to the Confederacy, in 1863 embraced the Union occupation of the town, very likely because under rebel administration business had nearly ground to a stop, and food and clothing shortages had been severely felt.[8]

[6] For railroads see Rothrock, *French Broad–Holston Country*, 108–12. For the city's secession vote see *Knoxville Daily Register*, June 11, 1861. On Presbyterian Church see Rothrock, *French Broad–Holston Country*, 144.

[7] Percy M. Pentecost, "A Corporate History of Knoxville, Tennessee, Before 1860" (M.A. thesis, Univ. of Tenn., 1946), 85–86.

[8] The best study of the Battle of Knoxville is Maury Klein, "The Knoxville Campaign," *Civil War Times Illustrated* 10 (Oct. 1971): 4–10, 42.

U. S. troops continued to hold Knoxville until the end of the Civil War, in spite of Confederate efforts in late 1863 to recapture the town and thereby reopen rail traffic to Richmond. That Confederate attempt, of which the important Battle of Fort Sanders was the climax, was described by one historian as "the most bungled, inept and ill-fated campaign in Confederate military annals." That battle, which saw southerners unsuccessfully attempt to carry out an ill-conceived assault on the earthworks of hastily completed Fort Sanders, not only wasted troops that the Confederacy could ill afford to lose but also kept the town essentially out of the war after 1863.[9]

After the war, some Knoxvillians with Unionist sympathies urged wholesale proscription and persecution of former rebels. But the majority seemed eager to put the conflict behind them. One hundred Unionists took an oath to eschew violence against former Confederates; several former rebels were able to regain their property after wartime confiscations; and the Ku Klux Klan, founded in West Tennessee, was relatively inactive in the Knoxville area. By 1867, when a serious flood threatened the town, former Confederates and Unionists worked together to save the Cumberland Avenue Bridge and provide assistance to the homeless.[10]

THE NEW SOUTH COMES TO KNOXVILLE

But if both sides were quick to put aside old animosities and grudges, that did not mean that Knoxvillians were willing to see the town return to the economic, social, and political ways of the Old South. For when the Confederacy fell at Appomattox, a lot more was destroyed than a government or an economic system built on slave labor. Also seriously weakened was the hold of the plantation aristocracy over the economic, political, social, and intellectual reins of the defeated section. In place of that aristocracy arose cadres of southern businessmen, merchants, bankers, and speculators eager to turn the South in new directions. These men had been present in the section for most of the nineteenth century, but the fall of the plantation aristocracy gave them both opportunity and power to put their ideas to work. Thus was born the New South movement, a movement that eventually found its most articulate spokesman and booster in Atlanta editor Henry Grady.

Advocates of the New South envisioned a section where bounteous natural resources, a virtually untapped labor pool, and capital investment (principally by northern and foreign speculators) could be brought together to industrialize and urbanize the South, make it less dependent on northern manufactured goods, and truly bring the South into the modern industrial

[9]Ibid., 4.
[10]Rothrock, *French Broad–Holston Country*, 141–47.

Knoxville, looking north from the Tennessee River

age. Bold and visionary, these men saw themselves as the southern counterparts of Rockefeller, Carnegie, and Morgan, and they dreamed of a new
order that would benefit both their section and themselves.[11]

But while bold and visionary, these New South boosters were also in-
tensely conservative. For one thing, the New South they envisioned demanded a kind of top-down planning and control not vastly different from
the hold plantation aristocrats had on the prewar section. Since northern
investors would not be lured to a South that either remained hostile to
"Yankees" or was so politically divided that "safe" political institutions
were unpredictable, New South advocates realized they would have to
control politics with an iron hand and beat back any political challenges from
the discredited plantation aristocracy, the white yeomen, or the newly
enfranchised blacks. Whites must be shown the benefits of industrialization
and political deference to their economic "betters," while blacks must
continue to possess their constitutional rights while tacitly agreeing not to
exercise them.[12]

In many ways Knoxville was in a perfect position to take advantage of the
New South movement. Rail connections, natural resources, and a potential
labor pool in the hinterland were all abundant; the elite of merchants, bankers, and professional men already had shown themselves to be accepting of
what became the New South creed; the rapid deterioration of Civil War
hostilities made the town attractive to northern investors; the black population was, by southern standards, comparatively small; the populace appeared to show little interest in politics, thus making elite control easier.
Indeed, to Knoxvillians and interested outsiders, it seemed that the once-
sleepy town possessed all the ingredients necessary to become a major city
of the New South.

In 1869 a local board of trade was formed under the leadership of Mas-
sachusetts native Perez Dickinson, and that same year the town's Industrial
Association was created to encourage the growth of extractive and manufacturing endeavors. Those few upper-class citizens (most of them former
Confederate sympathizers) who could not adjust to the New South movement were peacefully but unceremoniously eased aside. They were allowed
to retain their vaunted positions as arbiters of taste, fashion, and culture, but
they were now out of step with the town's new, dynamic vision.[13]

The postwar years saw Knoxville develop as a major southern commercial center. While the railroad undoubtedly was the key factor, also responsible for this achievement were the willingness of northerners to invest in

[11]Woodward, *Origins of the New South*, 107–41.
[12]Ibid., 107–74, 205–34.
[13]On Dickinson see *Daily Press and Herald*, May 4, 1869; Rothrock, *French Broad–
Holston Country*, 220, 411–12.

Gay Street, 1869
MCCLUNG HISTORICAL COLLECTION
KNOXVILLE–KNOX COUNTY PUBLIC LIBRARY

the town's commercial ventures and the spirit of dynamism that seems to have permeated the city. As the *Daily Chronicle* exulted in 1875, "Our merchant princes are increasing in number, and fortunes that a few years back would have been considered fabulous are now undoubted facts."[14] Unlike much southern booster rhetoric, the *Chronicle's* statement was fairly accurate. By 1874 the leading wholesaling firm of Cowan, McClung and Company (the state's largest taxpayer in 1867) had sales of $2 million annually, and approximately fifty other wholesaling houses in Knoxville each employed an average of twenty people. Former Union soldiers who had mustered-out in Knoxville—men like Hiram Chamberlain, A.J. Albers, and William Wallace Woodruff (the latter two names are still prominent in the city's wholesaling-retailing community)—also became prominent wholesalers and apparently were accepted into the town's elite with few difficulties. Indeed, a new urban elite was being formed in Knoxville, composed partly of northerners looking for business oppportunities, partly of prewar aristocrats who had been caught up in the new vision, and partly of Knoxvillians who had not been wealthy before the war but who recognized the town's postwar potential and moved to take advantage of it. But while Knoxville's New South elite was composed of several groups, ideologically it was homogeneous. All its members embraced the new spirit of economic expansion, unrestrained capitalism, and urban growth.[15]

By 1885 Knoxville was the fourth leading wholesaling center in the South, surpassed only by New Orleans, Atlanta, and Nashville, with an annual volume of business of between $15 and $20 million (three times that of manufacturing). Local merchants dealt principally in dry goods, groceries, boots and shoes, hardware, and machinery. Even more impressive, by 1896 the city was the South's third-largest wholesaler, with an annual dollar volume of approximately $50 million, a striking figure since at the time the nation was only beginning to emerge from the depression that had followed the Panic of 1893.[16]

Population growth mirrored the city's increased economic activity. Between 1860 and 1880 population more than doubled, from 3,704 in 1860 to a healthy 9,693 in 1880. Annexation of the area roughly south of Vine Avenue and east of Central in 1868 was responsible for only part of that growth, the majority of the increase being accounted for by the number of people moving into the city from the surrounding hinterland.[17]

[14]*Daily Chronicle*, Aug. ll, 1875.

[15]John Hope Franklin, *Reconstruction: After the Civil War*, in Daniel J. Boorstin, ed., *The Chicago History of American Civilization* (Chicago, 1961), 94–96; Lucile Deaderick, ed., *Heart of the Valley: A History of Knoxville, Tennessee* (Knoxville, 1976), 32–34.

[16]*Knoxville Market Annual* (Knoxville, 1908), 3–5, 24; Deaderick, ed., *Heart of the Valley*, 33–34, 47; Rothrock, *French Broad–Holston Country*, 222.

[17]U.S. Census 1860 and 1880.

The sources of this population growth merit more examination, since these in-migrants helped to shape the new city as much as did its elite. Most significant was the dramatic rise in the city's black population. In 1860 of Knoxville's 3,704 citizens, only 752 (20.3 percent) were black. When Union soldiers took Knoxville in 1863, blacks began to arrive in large numbers. And the end of the Civil War did not halt this flow, even though the recently formed Freedmen's Bureau counseled newly freed blacks to remain in the rural areas and not to glut Knoxville's then-small labor market. Commercial expansion in the postwar years provided jobs for blacks, many of whom found employment with the Knoxville and Ohio Railroad; the East Tennessee, Virginia and Georgia Railroad; the Knoxville Car Wheel Company; and Burr and Terry's Saw Mill. Of course, increased economic opportunities attracted still larger numbers of blacks, until by 1880 they numbered 3,149, or 32.5 percent of Knoxville's population. Since many were both employed and enfranchised, in burgeoning postwar Knoxville blacks held the potential for real economic and political power. In the New South atmosphere in which blacks were permitted to retain their political rights as long as they made no move to exercise them, whether they should use that power to better their collective lot was a dilemma that would plague Knoxville's blacks for years to come.[18]

While the number of blacks in Knoxville quadrupled between 1860 and 1880, the influx of whites from the surrounding hinterland was numerically even more impressive. Like their black counterparts, many of the white in-migrants were only marginally skilled and hence took low-wage jobs in the factories, wholesaling houses, and shops of the mushrooming city. Few had abandoned their Appalachian mores, their rough-and-tumble democratic politics, their fundamentalist religions, or their suspicion of their economic betters. Violence was widespread, taverns still far outnumbered churches, and homicide was a regular feature of the city's life.[19]

Barely noticeable at first in the thriving postwar commercial center was the rise of a new industrial order that surfaced soon after the Civil War but that was not fully appreciated until years later. Relying on northern capital and technological proficiency from outside the region, the industrialization of Knoxville soon supplemented the healthy commercial sector and further served as a magnet pulling labor out of the hills and hollows of Appalachia.

At the end of the Civil War, Knoxville had little that could be called industrial activity. The town could boast of only a few flour mills, furniture

[18]Alrutheus Ambush Taylor, *The Negro in Tennessee, 1865–1880* (Washington, D.C., 1941), 27, 30–35, 141–42. On enfranchisement and percentage of black voters see *Clinton Weekly Gazette*, Oct. 17, 1894, quoted in Gordon M. McKinney, "Southern Mountain Republicans and the Negro, 1865–1900," *Journal of Southern History* 41 (Nov. 1975): 512.

[19]On crime see Deaderick, ed., *Heart of the Valley*, 34–35, 38.

Knoxville Iron Company founded in 1867 by
Union veteran H. S. Chamberlain
(Photograph taken in the 1950s)

MCCLUNG HISTORICAL COLLECTION
KNOXVILLE–KNOX COUNTY PUBLIC LIBRARY

shops, saddleries, foundries, and other assorted small enterprises. But in 1867 Hiram S. Chamberlain, a native of Ohio and a Union Army officer who was mustered out of the service in Knoxville, founded the Knoxville Iron Company. Chamberlain, who had been Burnside's chief quartermaster during the Union occupation of Knoxville, was a shrewd businessman who recognized that abundant natural resources (coal, iron), good transportation facilities, a large potential labor pool, and the absence of anti-northern sentiment made Knoxville an ideal location for his enterprise. Using borrowed capital, he founded the Knoxville Iron Company, which eventually employed over 800 workers, mostly blacks and Welsh immigrants. The racially mixed work force lived close to the factory and each other (the Welsh in substantial Victorian homes and the blacks in modest dwellings) in the area soon known as Mechanicsville.[20]

The Knoxville Iron Company set patterns others would follow in the industrialization of Knoxville. Most enterprises were located on the northern and northwestern fringes of the growing city, where land was generally inexpensive and where access to the important railroad lines was easy. Housing was constructed around the factories or mills either by the industrialists themselves or by private developers. By the 1880s Knoxville's commercial center (the "downtown") was ringed on the northern and northwestern fringe by a collection of mill villages (Mechanicsville, Brookside Village) that continued to maintain characteristics of individual neighborhoods long after they had grown together as one city. Skilled labor usually was imported from outside, whereas the semiskilled and unskilled jobs went to black and white in-migrants. Coal was almost invariably the source of power.[21]

The 1880s witnessed Knoxville's greatest manufacturing boom. Between 1880 and 1887 alone, 97 new factories were built. In addition to iron mills and machine shops that processed iron into a multitude of finished products, cloth mills and furniture factories sprang up and prospered. And once the cloth mills came to Knoxville, it was only natural that a thriving apparel

[20]On Chamberlain see Franklin, *Reconstruction*, 94–96; Rothrock, *French Broad–Holston Country*, 313; Deaderick, ed., *Heart of the Valley*, 32. On Mechanicsville see Metropolitan Planning Commission, *Mechanicsville, Lonsdale, Beaumont Small Area Study* (Knoxville, 1976).

[21]*Knoxville Market Annual*, 3–5, 24. The marble companies were Knoxville Marble Company (1873), J.J. Craig Company (1886), Phoenix Marble (1885), W.H. Evans Company (1886), and East Tennessee Stone and Marble (1889). Foundries and iron companies established in the period include Clark Foundry and Machine (1881); W.J. Savage Mill and Machinery (1885); Southern Car Company (1881), which made car wheels for the railroads; Enterprise Machine Works (1886). Textile manufacturing included Knoxville Woolen Mills (1884) and Brookside Cotton Mills (1886). Lumber cutters and processors included D.M. Rose Sawmill (1880), which furnished 50,000 board feet per day; Scottish Carolina Timber and Land (1888); Knoxville Box and Keg (1872); and Knoxville Furniture (1882).

industry would follow. Coal companies were founded to provide power for the mills and factories and heat for residences (Knoxvillians having virtually denuded the outskirts of the town by the Civil War in their search for firewood). In addition to the fifteen coal companies, five marble companies also specialized in extracting raw materials from the area (thereby briefly giving the city the nickname "Marble City").

By 1900 heavy manufacturing and related enterprises had become a significant factor in Knoxville's economy. Capital investment in manufacturing had multiplied sixfold between 1870 and 1890, rising from $449,915 to $3,045,661, while the number of men, women, and children employed in manufacturing had risen even more dramatically, from 436 to 3,113. Indeed, by 1900 more Knoxvillians were engaged in manufacturing (30.6 percent of the labor force) than in commerce (29.5 percent), which had been the city's initial stimulus to economic growth after the Civil War. The value of goods manufactured annually in Knoxville had jumped from $923,211 in 1870 to $6,201,840 in 1899. Though the commercial sector still led in dollar volume, the percentage increases in manufacturing and the rising proportion of the labor force employed left little doubt that industrialization was Knoxville's wave of the future. Between 1900 and 1905 alone, manufactured goods had increased over 100 percent.[22]

Although the Panic of 1893 temporarily blunted the city's impressive economic growth, by the early years of the twentieth century the frenetic commercial and manufacturing activity of the preceding three decades was affecting other sectors of the city's economy. Bank clearings in 1905 were up 120.48 percent over those in 1900, having gone from $28,834,248.48 to $63,576,086.17. Those increases testified to the health of the city's ten banks, all of which had been organized after 1870, with four founded since 1890. Construction of new homes (over 5,000 built between 1895 and 1904, most of them in the latter years) was so impressive that as late as 1939 a Knoxville housing survey found that over 20 percent of all the city's houses had been built during that ten-year period. Forty companies were distributing coal by 1905; sales of shoes manufactured in the city totaled $4 million annually by 1908; cloth manufacturing was highest among any southern city; and dry goods and hardware sales were equally impressive. Truly, it appeared that all the optimistic prophecies of Knoxville's postwar boosters had come true.[23]

Part of this impressive growth in economic activity was serving the city's rapidly increasing population. By 1900 Knoxville's population had risen to

[22]*Knoxville Market Annual*, 3–5, 24; *U.S. Census*, 1870, 1880, and 1890.

[23]*Knoxville Market Annual* (Knoxville, 1908), 3–5, 24. On housing see *Commercial and Industrial Survey of Knoxville, Tennessee*, compiled for the Chamber of Commerce (Knoxville, 1939).

Gay Street, c. 1900

MCCLUNG HISTORICAL COLLECTION
KNOXVILLE–KNOX COUNTY PUBLIC LIBRARY

32,637, an increase partly accounted for by the annexations in 1883 of McGhee's Addition (later Mechanicsville) and in 1898 of the adjacent town of West Knoxville (earlier White's and Ramsey's Addition, later known as the Fort Sanders area) and the neighborhoods north of Baxter Avenue. The West Knoxville area was an especially welcome addition to the city, for during the latter years of the nineteenth century the wealthy postwar elite had increasingly abandoned its older residential neighborhoods in favor of newer, more opulent suburbs near the old Civil War redoubt of Fort Sanders. Here, magnificent late-Victorian residences were constructed, many of which, graced by wide porches and decorated with profusions of then-fashionable gingerbread, compared favorably with the most luxurious in the nation.[24]

Much of Knoxville's population increase, however, came from rural whites and blacks who came to the city to seek employment. Most were from the surrounding hinterland of East Tennessee; by 1900 the city's population was over 75 percent Tennessee-born, with Virginia (4.78 percent) and North Carolina (3.62 percent) natives a very distant second and third. Most of these recent arrivals were young, a fact that gave Knoxville's total population a youthful composition (in 1900, about one-third under fifteen and over 80 percent under forty-five). Whites brought with them traditional Appalachian mores, some of which (strong sense of family and kin, spirit of cooperation) aided their adjustment to urban living, while others (suspicion of government and authority, willingness to resort to violence, racism) made adjustment difficult. Illiteracy among white and black newcomers was high, with over one-third of the voting-age black males able neither to read nor to write. The low-paying jobs in the factories and railroad shops that most newcomers found meant that they tended to live perpetually on the edge of privation.[25]

THE NEW SOUTH AND THE URBAN BLACK

Rapid industrialization and population growth were hardly unmixed blessings for Knoxville or its inhabitants. The almost universal adoption of coal both for factories and residences gave the city a distinctly grimy, sooty appearance. Beyond the downtown area, street paving had been done only in some spots, and spring and fall rains left many Knoxvillians mud-splashed and dirty. Few trees softened the landscape, for the available timber had been used for fuel prior to the conversion to coal. Cows, accompanied by inevitable odors, still roamed the city streets, and Knoxville

[24]Knoxville Heritage, Inc., *Fort Sanders Walking Tour* (Knoxville, 1977).
[25]*Twelfth Census* (1900), tables 9, 30, 88.

*Stately homes such as this one on Clinch Avenue were built
in the Fort Sanders area in the 1880s and 1890s*

MCCLUNG HISTORICAL COLLECTION
KNOXVILLE–KNOX COUNTY PUBLIC LIBRARY

continually battled flies and diseases resulting from dirty streets, the lack of a sewer system, and contaminated water supplies. Not until the 1890s did the city have an adequate supply of clean water. As much as anything, Knoxville residents of the period remembered the dirt, coal dust, and unpleasant odors. For some, it was what they recollected as being the most conspicuous and universal characteristic of Knoxville at the turn of the century.[26]

More important for Knoxville's future than the city's physical griminess was the residential segregation by economic class that was beginning to divide the city. In the early days of the city's industrialization, factory owners, foremen, and workers had lived close to one another. Indeed, one can still see the architectural vestiges of this residential heterogeneity in the East Scott–Oklahoma Avenue area as well as around the Fourth and Gill neighborhood. But the increasing deterioration of the air and streets as well as a desire to separate themselves from the flood of Appalachian whites and blacks who some feared even as they needed their labor caused many of Knoxville's wealthier citizens to build fashionable enclaves like West Knoxville (Fort Sanders) on the fringes of the city. The extension of streetcar lines probably was the key force that uncorked the demographic bottle and allowed the "better sort" to escape to their more refined neighborhoods. Simultaneously, the demand for housing among the Appalachian newcomers meant that once-separated mill "villages" were beginning to grow together, merging into large working-class neighborhoods like Mechanicsville and the North Central Avenue area. In those neighborhoods, members of the elite might well be treated with great deference on a rare visit, but they were definitely traveling through areas that were no longer theirs. Increasing residential segregation became a fact of life that Knoxvillians would have to deal with for years to come.

The mixed blessings of industrialization, rapid population growth, and residential segregation by economic class were especially felt by the city's black population. Although industrialization had brought some economic gains for Knoxville's blacks, the New South notion of the politically docile black was an infuriating one that many blacks were eager to correct. In a city peopled with a visionary but conservative elite and a flood of Appalachian whites whose hostility to blacks only increased after they were forced to live and work close to them, Knoxville's blacks would certainly tread a dangerous path when they sought to challenge the New South code.

[26]Recollections of businessman-historian Russell Briscoe in address at Sequoyah Branch of Knoxville–Knox County Library, 1972. For problems in other cities see American Child Health Association, *A Health Survey of 86 Cities* (New York, 1925); Mazyck P. Ravenal, *A 3Half Century of Public Health* (New York, 1921). For somewhat later see the valuable *Knoxville's Health*, a monthly publication of the Bureau of Health, Dept. of Public Welfare, 1932–1940.

Blacks had begun to migrate to the town in significant numbers during the Civil War, while Union troops occupied the city. And after the war they continued to come. Seeking escape from rigid social codes as well as bleak economic prospects, area blacks ignored those who counseled them to remain on the land and not to be overly optimistic about economc or social opportunities in the cities. Once in Knoxville, most took comparatively low-paying jobs in railroad construction and shops, in the rapidly growing iron industry, in the marble quarries, and in local factories. With employers desperate for labor, it appeared at first that race would be less of a barrier to employment in the New South cities, and many blacks naively believed that the injustices and inequities of the Old South would be obliterated in the coal dust of the new age.[27]

In Knoxville such hopes were not entirely illusory. After the war the city's leaders seemed eager to assist blacks in their transition to freedom. Industrialist H.S. Chamberlain spoke in glowing terms of blacks employed in the iron industry, praising their good work habits, their eagerness for education, their abilities to take on responsible positions, and their penchant for saving money to purchase their own homes. Knoxville blacks moved rapidly to organize their own churches (prohibited before the Civil War), fraternal orders, self-improvement societies, and fire companies. By the 1880s the city could boast of black policemen, lawyers, and businessmen. Moreover, whites helped to provide educational opportunities which, it was hoped, would enable Knoxville's blacks to rise from slavery. Emily Austin of Philadelphia used money collected in the North to found schools for blacks. Austin-East High School is named for her. In 1875 the Presbyterian Church founded a school for blacks, ironically located near the Confederate defenses of General Longstreet; this school would develop into the present Knoxville College. Meanwhile, white political leaders seemed determined to maintain racial peace in the growing city. To do so was no mean feat, since working-class whites and blacks were thrown into close work and residential proximity.[28]

Despite these advances, however, some local black leaders were disap-

---

[27]Blacks who migrated to southern cities generally came from the surrounding rural areas. See Homer L. Hitt, "Peopling the City: Migration," in Rupert B. Vance and Nicholas J. Demerath, eds., *The Urban South* (Chapel Hill, 1954), 60. On migration of blacks to cities see George E. Haynes, "The Movement of Negroes from the Country to the City," *The Southern Workman* 42 (Apr. 1913): 230–36; Taylor, *The Negro in Tennessee, 1865–1880*, 39–35. Black population in Knoxville increased from 752 persons in 1860 (20.3% of the total population) to 2,609 in 1870 (30.1%) to 3,149 in 1880 (32.5%). Principal industrial employers of blacks in Knoxville included the Knoxville and Ohio Railroad; the Knoxville Iron Company; Knoxville Rolling Mills; the East Tennessee, Virginia and Georgia Railroad; Knoxville Foundry and Machine Company; Burr and Terry Saw Mill; Knoxville Leather Company; and Knoxville Car Wheel Company. Taylor, *The Negro in Tennessee*, 142.

[28]Rothrock, *The French Broad–Holston Country*, 316–19.

Knoxville College, probably the Class of 1907

BECK CULTURAL EXCHANGE CENTER

pointed with what they saw as the pitifully slow progress being made. Since black voters represented over one-third of the city's voting population throughout the late nineteenth century, the potential existed for blacks to make their disappointment felt at the polls. Some black leaders proposed that the people do just that.[29]

After their enfranchisement, most southern blacks had voted Republican, seeing that party as the party of Lincoln, emancipation, and the Freedmen's Bureau. But by the mid-1870s, the national Republican party had turned in a different direction, a direction dramatized by the barely successful presidential campaign of Rutherford B. Hayes in 1876. To Republicans, it was a matter of political necessity, for as southern states one by one returned to the Union, the Republican party feared that it would become again a minority party to be regularly trampled on by the Democratic majority. Republicans began to change political direction, hoping to embrace the new businessmen of the New South. With that goal in mind and less willing to stand at the deteriorating forefront of social and political reform (especially with regard to the freedmen), the party of Lincoln and emancipation became the party of business and business conservatism.[30]

Many black leaders in Knoxville, as throughout the South, sensed the Republican party's change of direction. Republicans, they reasoned, might still be eager for their votes but less willing to alienate New South business interests by trading those votes for political support of Negro economic and social objectives. The only solution, black leaders felt, was to declare independence of both major political parties, and, with Democrats and Republicans alike, to barter ballots for programs in the interests of the freedmen.

This revised approach by blacks has been labeled the "New Departure." In Knoxville it was signaled in 1876 when black attorney William F. Yardley announced that he would run for governor of Tennessee as an independent. Yardley was thirty-two years old in 1876, a free mulatto who had been born in Knox County in 1844, read law on his own, and passed the bar examination to become a respected criminal lawyer and local political figure. Yardley had no chance of victory, and very likely he knew it. But the Knoxville lawyer used the gubernatorial campaign to dramatize blacks' declaration of independence from the Republican party. Yardley spent most of his time attacking the Republicans. Blacks had naively and patiently voted Republican, he asserted, and had received little in return for their political fealty. Not surprisingly, Yardley was swamped.[31]

[29]Blacks represented 35.6% of the total registered voters in 1894. *Clinton Weekly Gazette*, Oct. 17, 1894, quoted in McKinney's "Southern Mountain Republicans and the Negro," 512.

[30]Especially good on Republican strategy is Vincent P. DeSantis, *Republicans Face the Southern Question—The New Departure Years, 1877–1897* (Baltimore, 1959).

[31]*Daily Tribune*, Sept. 2, 1876; Rothrock, *French Broad–Holston Country*, 324–25; Deaderick, ed., *Heart of the Valley*, 41.

William F. Yardley

BECK CULTURAL EXCHANGE CENTER

To many black leaders in Knoxville, however, Yardley's campaign was less a realistic political battle than it was the cannon signaling the New Departure. In 1877 Yardley again stood at the forefront of Knoxville's blacks, urging them to move independently of the Republican party in their efforts to secure the right to sit on juries. In addition, blacks began regularly to form committees in the 1870s and 1880s to interview candidates for local offices. For example, in 1888 a committee of black leaders met separately with both Democratic and Republican candidates for mayor. The Reverend Job Lawrence, a black minister of the Shiloh Presbyterian Church and probably a member of the committee, subsequently attacked Republicans for ignoring blacks except at election time. "We are," Lawrence asserted, "no more free than in the days of bondage."[32]

Black support of mayoral incumbent James C. Luttrell, Jr., undoubtedly was an important factor in the Democrat's reelection. In return for that support, Luttrell pressured aldermen under his control to appoint Reverend Lawrence to the Knoxville Board of Education. The appointment was greeted by an immediate public explosion. The board itself was loathe to let Lawrence sit as a member, never informing him of meeting dates and once ejecting him from a meeting. One local editorialist fanned the fires by commenting that Lawrence's behavior in forcing himself on the previously all-white school board "may be an indication of what he [Lawrence] might do should he take a notion to visit the Girls' High School." Ultimately the board sued to remove Lawrence, who lost an appeal to the State Supreme Court. Subsequently Lawrence probably left the city; at any rate, he was not in Knoxville in 1893. In 1894 alarmed white political leaders from both parties quietly gerrymandered Knoxville's blacks into virtual political impotence, and the New Departure—at least in Knoxville—was dead.[33]

THE RHETORIC AND REALITY OF THE NEW SOUTH

In the midst of these physical, social, and political problems Knoxville's New South advocates continued to maintain that all was well. Large retailers, merchants, factory owners, and large real estate holders were never without statistics that seemed to prove the city's great progress and even greater potential. Boosters even used the great fire of 1897 (which destroyed

[32] On Yardley see *Knoxville Daily Tribune*, Dec. 29, 1877. On Lawrence see ibid., Dec. 24, 1887. An excellent account of black political involvement in Knoxville is Sally Ripatti, "Black Political Involvement in Late Nineteenth Century Knoxville" (unpub. manuscript, 1976, in author's possession).

[33] Ripatti, "Black Political Involvement," 10–18. See also *Daily Tribune*, July 14, 1888. On gerrymandering see *Clinton Weekly Gazette*, Oct. 17, 1894, quoted (complete with ward totals) in McKinney, "Southern Mountain Republicans and the Negro," 512.

The "Million Dollar Fire," 1897

MCCLUNG HISTORICAL COLLECTION
KNOXVILLE–KNOX COUNTY PUBLIC LIBRARY

Main entrance to the Appalachian Exposition, 1913

MCCLUNG HISTORICAL COLLECTION
KNOXVILLE–KNOX COUNTY PUBLIC LIBRARY

a number of businesses on the east side of Gay Street, roughly north of Union Avenue), dubbing it the "Million Dollar Fire" and pointing to it proudly both as an example of the city's wealth and as a testament to the city's regenerative powers. To serve as showcases for the city's progress, in 1910, 1911, and 1913 these boosters, led by such members of the local elite as William J. Oliver, Lawrence Tyson, and William M. Goodman, sponsored regional expositions at Chilhowee Park that aped the self-congratulatory and economically stimulating earlier expositions of Chicago, Buffalo, St. Louis, and Atlanta. All the expositions were intended to dramatize Knoxville's economic vitality, its potential for commercial expansion, and the physical beauty of the surrounding countryside. Although regional agriculture maintained a prominent place at the most famous of these expositions, the Appalachian Exposition of 1910 (for which impressive buildings were constructed that ultimately became the principal buildings of the Tennessee Agricultural and Industrial Fair), undoubtedly Knoxville's New South advocates were more interested in displaying the city's commercial and industrial prowess.[34]

Yet, even as Knoxville's architects of the New South continued to boast of the city's progress and potential, fragmentary evidence suggests that not all Knoxvillians shared the boosters' optimism. Between 1900 and 1910 the city's population growth was an anemic 11.7 percent, a rate of growth less than one would expect from natural increase alone. In the same period, areas surrounding the city were experiencing dramatic growth rates. The population in Knox County (excluding the city) increased 38.8 percent, until by 1910 almost 40 percent of the county's total population was living in the suburbs of Lonsdale, Oakwood, Park City, Mountain View, and Looney's Bend (later Sequoyah Hills). Even more startling was the fact that the city's proportion of young people (under fifteen) decreased by roughly 4 percent between 1900 and 1910. These statistics suggest that people—and especially younger people with young children—were leaving the city to seek homes either in the surrounding county or in regions beyond.[35]

Undoubtedly, a significant proportion of those who left Knoxville were black, for between 1900 and 1910 the city's black population increased by less than 300 people (from 7,359 to 7,638). This meager increase meant that the percentage of Knoxville residents who were black continued to decline (from 30.1 percent in 1870 to 21.0 percent in 1910), eroding blacks' political influence and making it harder for them to secure a voice in local political decisions. Poor economic opportunities seem to have combined with the

---

[34]Rothrock, *French Broad–Holston Country*, 215–16; Deaderick, *Heart of the Valley*, 45, 47–50.

[35]*Twelfth Census* (1900) and *Thirteenth Census* (1910).

increasing hostility of neighboring whites to drive blacks from Knoxville in fairly large numbers. By 1918, when black educator, lawyer, and Republican political figure Charles W. Cansler recognized the significance of this black exodus, the trend had been going on for some time.[36]

In addition to the very modest growth rate, other signs suggested that the euphoria of local boosters masked a situation in which all was not well. Even among the elite itself (those industrialists, merchants, lawyers, and professional men who had risen to prominence after the Civil War) there appeared a growing conservatism, a loss of dynamism, and an unwillingness to provide top-down direction for the city. Even as they trumpeted the accomplishments of the New South city, their exodus to newer neighborhoods in the west symbolized a general abrogation of responsibility for the city this elite had done so much to create. What was more serious, elite manufacturers gradually embraced the notion of exchanging long-term growth and vitality for short-term profits by not replacing obsolete machinery or methods. Indeed, it was as if their political conservatism (so typical of New South elites) had infected their economic and social ideas as well.

Those of the elite who fought against this growing conservatism were likely to be newcomers recently accepted into the city's exclusive circles. Representative of these newcomers was William J. Oliver, a native of Indiana who by 1905 had moved to Knoxville and founded the Oliver Manufacturing Company. Also in the construction business, Oliver built the Clinch Avenue viaduct and by 1909 had completed the rail connections to Sevierville later known as the Smoky Mountain Railroad. An aggressive New South booster, he was a key figure in the organization of the regional expositions of 1910, 1911, and 1913 and was the man who persuaded his political friend Theodore Roosevelt (whom he later followed into the Progressive or Bull Moose party) to visit the 1910 exposition. For all his energy, however, Oliver seemed unable to arrest the conservative shift among his fellow elite members and later criticized them openly. He charged that many actually discouraged growth and new businesses, preferring the city as it was rather than as it could become.[37]

A good indication of the growing conservatism of most of the city's elite was its stand on the prohibition issue. From the 1870s on, the conflict over the prohibition of liquor sales had been a central issue in Tennessee politics. Little by little the prohibitionists had triumphed until, by 1907, the whole state was dry except for the four largest cities. In that year the state legislature made it possible for these cities to redraw their charters of incorporation

---

[36]Ibid. On Cansler see Lester C. Lamon, ed., "Document—Charles W. Cansler to the Honorable Tom C. Rye, Governor of Tennessee, February, 1918," *Journal of Negro History* 57 (Oct. 1972): 407–14.

[37]Deaderick, ed., *Heart of the Valley*, 48–49, 590.

so as to eliminate the sale of liquor. The redrawn charters would have to be approved by the voters of the respective cities.[38]

Though campaigns were mounted by the Women's Christian Temperance Union (WCTU), the Anti-Saloon League, and other groups in all four cities, Knoxville was the only one that responded. In Knoxville the combined forces of the WCTU, the fundamentalist churches, and the Republican party (which had embraced prohibition statewide as a vote-getting device) proved extremely strong. Yet the elite, while continuing to slake its own thirst in exclusive suburbs and private clubs, seems to have done little or nothing to stop the prohibitionists' rout. Some of them even welcomed prohibition as a way to prevent working-class whites and blacks from securing strong drink, believing as they did that whiskey only encouraged them to be more vicious than they already were.

Those who stood against prohibitionists' attacks and elite inertia were overwhelmed. Mayor Samuel Gordon Heiskell, along with most of his Democratic political comrades, opposed prohibition in Knoxville. Heiskell, a city and state officeholder since 1884, had been a longtime friend of education, Negro rights, and the New South ideology. In spite of the obvious danger to his political career, he attacked the prohibitionists, asserting that the annual $30,000 brought in from the saloon tax was used to support public education and that the loss of that revenue would mean that property taxes would have to be raised to balance the loss. Such an argument had little effect on the prohibitionists. Religious excitement, Republican vote-getting tactics, and the determination to "dry out" the working-class white and black neighborhoods easily carried the day by a vote of 4,150 to 2,255. The charter revision was approved and Knoxville was dry.[39]

The elite's growing unwillingness to become involved in the economic, social, and political issues had almost disastrous results for the city. Racial hostility, never far from the surface, now ran virtually unchecked, as it did in several American cities—north and south—in the early twentieth century. Though the residential proximity of blacks and Appalachian whites had provided a potentially explosive situation for years, the civic-commercial elite traditionally had been sympathetic to black aspirations and had exercised its influence to maintain racial harmony. But between 1870 and 1920, while that elite's power was waning and it was becoming more conservative and insulated, Knoxville's black population more than quadrupled (though the years after 1900 had seen a drastic decline in black migration). Now blacks spilled over into previously all-white neighborhoods, providing the tinder that awaited but one spark to set it aflame.

[38]Paul H. Bergeron, *Paths of the Past: Tennessee, 1770–1970* (Knoxville, 1979), 84.

[39]Ibid., 84; Deaderick, ed., *Heart of the Valley*, 106–7. On Heiskell's defense see *Sentinel*, Feb. 9, 1907.

Samuel G. Heiskell

REPRINTED FROM *Southern Review*, MAY 1898

In August 1919 the uneasy peace was broken. When police arrested Maurice Mayes, a mulatto who reportedly had shot and killed a white woman in an attempted robbery, many whites reacted with anger and alarm. Although Mayes had been quietly moved to Chattanooga, a mob stormed the Knoxville jail, freed several white prisoners, emptied the jail's whiskey storage room (where since prohibition confiscated whiskey had been kept), and demolished both the jail and the sheriff's adjoining home. From there the mob lumbered toward the corner of Vine and Central avenues, where it was rumored that armed blacks were gathering. On their way, the whites broke into several businesses, principally to acquire firearms. Even though guardsmen of the Tennessee Fourth Infantry had arrived on the scene, shooting broke out, with soldiers and white rioters firing at blacks and the blacks returning fire. More soldiers arrived the next day and peace was restored.[40]

Although the Knoxville riot was an exceedingly minor one compared with the racial violence that shook other American cities in the summer of 1919, Knoxville's elite was stunned. In its eyes the city had been a model of good race relations in the New South. Mayor John E. McMillan had denounced the Ku Klux Klan. Black school principal and political figure Charles W. Cansler recently had been honored by the city and the Colored Free Library had been opened in 1918. For years blacks and whites had lived and worked near one another. Suddenly, the elite felt, the city was falling apart.

But Knoxville's elite had badly misgauged the situation. Rural whites who had migrated from the Appalachian hinterlands had had a hard time adjusting to the city's regimented way of life. In industries like the Knoxville Iron Company and the Southern Railway, they had been forced into proximity with blacks, whom they had already loathed. Residential segregation, a regular feature of American urban life, had been breaking down under the pressure of black population growth. Moreover, the early years of the twentieth century had been anxious economic times for Knoxville. To maintain high profits, many of the city's increasingly conservative manufacturing elite had failed to replace obsolete or rundown equipment. Ultimately some of these factories, including the Knoxville Woolen Mills, which was the South's largest factory of its type, had been forced to close. Those closings, plus the fact that the city's working-age population had grown faster than the number of jobs, had caused much anxiety and discontent. Most likely this frustration had found its vent in the heightened racial tension of the World War I era.[41]

[40]Lester C. Lamon, "Tennessee Race Relations and the Knoxville Riot of 1919," East Tennessee Historical Society *Publications* 41 (1969): 67–85.

[41]William C. Ross, *A Scrapbook for My Grandchildren* (New York, 1941), 47–48.

Maurice Mayes

BECK CULTURAL EXCHANGE CENTER

Gay Street, c. World War I

In the face of all these realities, the rhetoric of Knoxville's New South spokesmen seemed hollow indeed. Physical griminess, economic slowdown, modest population growth, residential segregation by class and race, the growing conservatism of a large segment of the elite, and racial problems together signaled that if the New South had arrived in Knoxville, the benefits it brought to the city clearly had been mixed. For those so optimistic as to refuse to see reality, the city's 1917 annexation of approximately 22 square miles of Knox County (including the areas of Lonsdale, Mountain View, Park City, Oakwood, South Knoxville, and Looney's Bend [Sequoyah Hills]) sufficiently masked the city paltry population growth so as to make booster rhetoric plausible, if not entirely believable.[42]

THE POLITICS OF RHETORIC AND REALITY

In many ways, local politics mirrored the city's economic and social problems. New South boosters had advocated a new commercial-industrial order that demanded a strong measure of economic and political control from above. But the influx of blacks and Appalachian whites not only presented severe economic and social problems but also strongly challenged this notion of political deference. Their traditional suspicion of their "betters" combined with their distrust of government and political authority in general caused them to resist political control and planning from the top.

Those still active among Knoxville's elite seized on the general philosophy of the nationwide Progressive movement of the early twentieth century. Though generally—and correctly—labeled a major American reform movement (touching, as it did, issues of anti-trust, railroad regulation, pure foods and drugs, working hours and conditions), progressivism also proposed governmental reforms that would eliminate corruption and undue popular passions by removing government from the direct control of the people through independent commissions and nonelective officials. Hence, though ostensibly democratic, in many ways progressivism was anything but that.[43] As was the case in many if not most southern cities, those movements, political and efficiency-oriented, that were called "progressive" served essentially to perpetuate the ills of black urban populations and assure their political impotence. Knoxville was merely a striking example of the tensions created in this process.

[42]*U.S. Census*, 1910 and 1920; Deaderick, ed., *Heart of the Valley*, 109, 115.

[43]For two interesting analyses of progressivism see Robert H. Wiebe, *Businessmen and Reform: A Study of the Progressive Movement* (Cambridge, Mass., 1962), and Gabriel Kolko, *The Triumph of Conservatism: A Reinterpretation of American History, 1900–1916* (Glencoe, Ill., 1963).

Not surprisingly, the portion of Knoxville's elite that had not withdrawn from the public arena enthusiastically embraced this aspect of progressivism (though they often frowned on some of its other reform objectives). Believing that changes in the structure of the city's government both would bring forth businesslike efficiency and honesty and would lessen the potential threat of a political uprising from below, in 1912 this civic-minded elite group supported a change by which the city abandoned government by a mayor and alderman in favor of government by five commissioners. Each commissioner was the head of a department of the local government: public affairs, accounts and finance, public safety, streets and public improvements, and parks and public property. All were to be elected at large, insuring that racial or economic groupings by wards could have little effect on election outcomes.[44]

But the commission form of government quickly proved ineffectual. The nonelite resented the new government, since it made it more difficult for them to bring political pressure to bear on the "nonpolitical" commissioners in matters of political favors, jobs, and neighborhood improvements. Too, the 1917 annexation had not only added tax revenues to the city's coffers but also put such severe financial strains on the commissioners to provide city services that the new government rapidly was plunged into debt. Finally, the combination of executive and legislative functions in the five-man commission made overseeing the city's government a difficult task. Graft was uncovered in the awarding of paving and garbage-collection contracts and in the administration of the city hospital and water supply.

At last, fraud became so widespread (even election fraud was blatant) that in 1923 the active portion of the elite and an aroused middle-class citizenry altered Knoxville's government once again, discarding the commission form and replacing it with the "incorruptible" city manager–council type of government. The city manager form was popular among Progressives, for it emphasized efficiency, honesty, and the appearance of democracy while the real power remained in the hands of the nonelected manager. Although the office of mayor was ultimately reinstated, that position was largely an honorary post that went automatically to the councilman-at-large candidate with the highest vote total. In theory the elected council set broad general policies and the city manager administered those policies nonpolitically.[45]

The first city manager hired by the new council, in 1923, was former Knoxvillian and professional city manager Louis Brownlow. Brownlow was the quintessential city manager. A man of both vision and innovative ideas, he measured his successes and failures in terms of statistics and

---

[44]Deaderick, ed., *Heart of the Valley*, 111–12.

[45]Blaine A. Brownell, *The Urban Ethos in the South, 1920–1930* (Baton Rouge, 1975), 107; City Council Minute Book 10 (1923), 15, 86; Deaderick, ed., *Heart of the Valley*, 113–14.

Louis Brownlow (far left) with his cabinet, 1926

REPRINTED FROM *A Passion for Anonimity*
BY LOUIS BROWNLOW BY THE UNIVERSITY OF
CHICAGO PRESS

physical and fiscal changes, and he had little patience with politicians and what he considered the uninformed public. Although one volume of his autobiography is titled *A Passion for Anonymity*, Brownlow was anything but anonymous as he fought to overcome what he saw as Knoxville's lethargy and hostility to change as well as the people he considered to be the city's political neanderthals.[46]

It is not surprising that Brownlow, in spite of many accomplishments, saw his brief stay in Knoxville as essentially a failure. By 1926 he was being harassed continually by political pressure groups and a hostile city council and was driven to a nervous breakdown and ultimate resignation. Yet one cannot dismiss Brownlow easily, for his failure is a key to understanding the politics of the New South city. By World War I the conservatism of the post–Civil War Knoxville elite had become so pronounced and pervasive that more energetic newcomers to its circles (like Oliver and Heiskell, among others) seemed anomalous. Though they undoubtedly had the power, few had the inclination to become politically active in the rough-and-tumble Knoxville political arena. At the same time, those whites and blacks who had entered Knoxville to seek factory employment selected as their political spokesmen and champions men reminiscent of the rural Appalachian political styles they so fondly remembered. Fiercely democratic with a large streak of egalitarianism, these voters, through their spokesmen (whom the elite often characterized as demagogues), voiced their anger and frustration over their collective lot and their abiding suspicion of their "betters."[47]

Brownlow's principal antagonist during his brief tenure as city manager was Lee Monday, a city councilman who represented South Knoxville almost continuously from 1923 through 1939. Friend and enemy alike recognized that Monday was the voice on the Knoxville City Council of the white Appalachian workers, a man who articulated their fears. A sagacious politician, Monday became the most powerful person on the council less through his oratory than through political arrangements and deals made with some other councilmen, a kind of political horse-trading at which he was most adroit.

Of Monday, Brownlow recalled:

He was a hillbilly and he gloried in it. He was a roughneck and he knew it. He dressed the part and looked it. He was an orator in the good old mountain fashion, and he knew that too. Most of the time nearly every council meeting was taken up by his oratorical displays. It was fre-

---

[46]Louis Brownlow, *A Passion for Anonymity*, vol. 2 of *The Autobiography of Louis Brownlow* (Chicago, 1958), 190–97.

[47]Ibid., 190–97; interview with Lee S. Greene, Emeritus Professor of Political Science, Univ. of Tennessee, Knoxville, Feb. 15, 1977.

Lee Monday

MCCLUNG HISTORICAL COLLECTION
KNOXVILLE–KNOX COUNTY PUBLIC LIBRARY

quently difficult to understand exactly what he was talking about, but one knew, whatever the words, he instinctively was talking for the South Knoxvillians against all and sundry. He was the representative of his district and he was the representative of his clan, the East Tennesseans. He was representative of that top-of-the-voice screamology of East Tennessee mountain politics, and rarely in either his speeches or in the council or in the diatribes which my ears suffered when he called at my office did he ever depart from his own clear consciousness of his place in the scheme of things.[48]

As Monday saw it, his "place in the scheme of things" was to echo the thoughts and fears of the once-voiceless white working class against the city's "better sort." He was skeptical of Brownlow's concept of an active city government which, in addition to providing basic services for both the old city and the area annexed in 1917, sought to make recreation programs, regulate plumbers and electricians, and plan for future growth and development in the public sphere. He opposed the tax increases Brownlow demanded (a 16-percent increase during Brownlow's brief tenure), darkly warning of wasted monies and the city manager's reckless and extravagant schemes. More than once he accused Brownlow of heaping taxes on the working people so the elite could be better served and further enriched.

Fighting back, Brownlow's allies on the city council censured Monday for his attacks on the city manager. At the same time they tried to blunt Monday's opposition to tax increases by declaring a 10-percent tax dividend. But Monday would not be silenced. Dubbing Brownlow "King Louis I," he pilloried the city manager for his proposal of a large bond issue to build a new water plant, mocked his acquisition of the Deaf and Dumb Asylum for a new city hall as shamefully wasteful, and kept up a withering barrage on Brownlow's friends in the welfare department and on the new planning commission. In a special recall election in 1926, Monday campaigned beyond his district for anti-Brownlow city council candidates, the results of which deadlocked the council between pro-Brownlow and pro-Monday candidates. During that election Monday distributed a graphic poster that showed Brownlow and his allies as baby pigs sucking the teats of their city government "mother." Sensing the recall election results as a mandate against tax increases, an active city government, and change, Brownlow saw the handwriting on the wall and resigned.[49]

Knoxville's two attempts at governmental reform in the twentieth century essentially ended in failure (though the city manager–council form limped along ineffectually until the 1940s). While most members of the business

---

[48]Brownlow, *A Passion for Anonymity*, 190.
[49]Ibid., 197.

A typical election night, 1920s

MCCLUNG HISTORICAL COLLECTION
KNOXVILLE–KNOX COUNTY PUBLIC LIBRARY

elite seem to have favored the status quo of limited government, few changes, and low taxes, their lethargy was reinforced by the political ideology of Appalachian in-migrants for whom taxes symbolized urbanization and an attendant loss of independence. At the same time, spokesmen of these white working-class men and women opposed any efforts to make the city government less democratic by placing more power in the hands of nonelected officials. Therefore, while Knoxville's politics were often rough-and-tumble and vicious, even occasionally corrupt, they were nevertheless democratic and reflected the conservative sentiments of both the elite and the working classes.

Politically it was necessary to keep taxes as low as possible and to secure needed services or improvements through deficit spending and by issuing long-term bonds. Hence, by 1930 Knoxville's per capita net indebtedness was nearly twice that of any other Tennessee city, and debt servicing consumed increasingly large chunks of the city's operating capital. In 1930 the cost of city government was the highest among the state's major municipalities, even though some were almost twice as large as Knoxville. Therefore, as other cities in the nation and in the New South began considering schemes for improved services, urban renewal, and general beautification, a combination of conservative politics and poor finances kept Knoxville from responding to its own opportunities. Indeed, by the time John Gunther visited the city in 1945, Knoxville's inability to transform itself into a modern city was apparent. Although the city commissioned several plans and studies, Knoxville seemed incapable of bringing any of the grand schemes to fruition.[50]

THE FRAGMENTATION OF THE 1920s

Students of the 1920s have recognized for a long time that the period between the end of World War I and the Crash of 1929 was considerably more than an epoch of flappers, movie idols, bootleg gin, and the lost generation of Fitzgerald and Hemingway. Beneath that surface of prosperity and gaiety were profound economic and social problems that lent an air of both fear and desperation to the decade. Urbanization, demographic changes, and economic problems created a kind of fragmentation of the society, a fragmentation that even today has not been totally erased.

Knoxville was deeply affected by this fragmentation. As we have already seen, Knoxville in the 1920s was the scene of bitter political battles between those espousing opposing ideas of Knoxville's problems and of the role the city's government should play in addressing those problems. At the same

[50]On debt see Rothrock, *French Broad–Holston Country*, 184–85.

Gay Street, 1920s

MCCLUNG HISTORICAL COLLECTION
KNOXVILLE–KNOX COUNTY PUBLIC LIBRARY

time, residential segregation both by class and by race (a trend that had been going on for some time) seemed to accelerate, further fragmenting the city both socially and culturally. Having witnessed Brownlow's fate, those who might have been inclined to offer Knoxvillians other options remained silent.

As it was throughout the nation in the 1920s, Knoxville on the surface appeared to be a thriving New South city, a city whose glories were still in the future. In 1930 Knoxville's population reached 105,802, up from 77,818 a decade before—an impressive 36-percent increase. To serve this mushrooming population, over 6,123 houses were built in the city between 1920 and 1929; building permits reached a peak in the 1927–1928 period, with over 1,200 new construction projects, averaging over $6 million in value, begun each year. If taxes were kept so low as to be unable to provide basic services, that appeared to be the way most people wanted it, preferring instead to defer payments through deficit spending and bonded indebtedness. Even more noteworthy, a relatively high proportion of Knoxvillians and Knox Countians owned their own homes in 1930, and the city's population was a young society, with over 30 percent under fourteen years old and a full 82.93 percent under forty-five. Indeed, every statistic—from the number of telephones installed to the number of civic club members to the county's impressively low illiteracy—seemed to add weight to the assertion that Knoxville finally had "arrived."[51]

Private developers sensed the elite's need for insulation from the city and responded accordingly. In the 1920s several plans were hatched for ostentatious suburban developments in the western sections of the city, those areas annexed in 1917. In 1925 an out-of-state developer bought a large tract in Looney's Bend, renamed the area Sequoyah Hills, and made plans to sell lots to affluent citizens fleeing the core city. Nearby developments like Talahi maintained the upper-class flavor of the area, with all house plans submitted for approval and with rigid restrictions on grounds and service courts. Parks, fountains, gardens, and impressive stone edifices were designed to give the area both natural beauty and exclusivity. "Today a great

[51]Population and age distribution can be found in the *Fifteenth Census*, 1930. Building permit figures are from the records of the Knoxville Building Inspector, which are summarized in the 1934 reports in the TVA Technical Library (as are statistics on telephone installations and membership in civic organizations). Home ownership data come from the abstract of the *Fifteenth Census*, 1930, p. 436. Fully 40.6% of the homes in the city were owned in 1930, up 0.2% from 1920. County figures show an even greater stability, with 45.6% of the families owning their own homes in 1930 (47.3% of white and 32.6% of black). These figures are higher than for families in Shelby, Hamilton, or Davidson counties in 1930, and better by 8.5% than the state's average. As for illiteracy, 4.7% of Knox Countians were illiterate in 1930, down from 6.9% in 1920 and fourth lowest of any county in the state. Surrounding counties all had higher illiteracy figures in 1930: Union (9.9%), Anderson (8.1%), Blount (6.8%), Roane (7.8%), Sevier (9.3%), Rhea (6.3%), and Loudon (8.0%).

city is built close by," the Talahi developers boasted: "Near at hand is a busy artery of traffic [Kingston Pike] to and from that city, ten minutes away. . . . But in TALAHI's virgin forest, as in long years past, nature rules supreme. Its charm has not been subject to ruinous exploitation. On the contrary, the creators of this community have preserved for all time its natural beauty, adding to it only splendid adaptations of the landscape architect."[52]

Beneath the surface of economic vitality and developing elite suburbs, however, lurked disturbing demographic and economic trends. Most striking was the massive exodus of whites, both elite and working class, from the center (pre-1917) city. They were replaced not by other white in-migrants, as had been the case previously, but instead by blacks who were moving into the center city both from outlying wards and from black agrarian settlements beyond the county and state. This white exodus accounted for absolute white population declines between 1920 and 1930 in the pre-1917 city, Wards One through Nine (from the central business district northward to approximately Moses Avenue). Ward Five (east of Gay and bordered on north and south by Commerce and Church streets, respectively) experienced a dramatic 77.88-percent drop in white population during this period. Simultaneously, black population increased in eight of these nine wards during the 1920s and by 1930 accounted for over half the population of wards Three and Five. Between 1920 and 1930, Ward One (east of Gay along the Tennessee River) recorded a 247-percent jump in black population, with four of the other eight center-city wards experiencing more than a 32-percent increase.[53]

Why did so many blacks move into Knoxville so soon after the racial troubles of 1919? First, in the 1920s hard times were forcing many marginal farmers—white and black—off their traditional homesteads. Without land, the farmers had nowhere to go but the city. In addition, some of the blacks who migrated to the center city in the 1920s came from other city wards (Seventeen, Eighteen, Twenty, Twenty-one, and Twenty-three all experi-

---

[52] Mutual Development Company, *Talahi* [promotional literature] (Knoxville, 1929).

[53] The *Fourteenth Census* (1920) and *Fifteenth Census* (1930) indicate that the racial composition of central Knoxville changed rapidly in the 1920s:

WARD	WHITE POP., 1920–1930	BLACK POP., 1920–1930
1	−29.19%	+247.25%
2	−19.24	+ 4.17
3	−67.89	+98.00
4	− 9.56	+10.32
5	−77.88	+41.84
6	−29.66	+15.18
7	−14.93	+32.30
8	−27.28	+18.78
9	−15.69	+40.30

Edgewood A.M.E. Zion Church, 1926

BECK CULTURAL EXCHANGE CENTER

"The Bottom," a black residential district in the inner city, 1930s

BECK CULTURAL EXCHANGE CENTER

enced absolute declines in black population during the decade). Made anxious by the 1919 incidents, blacks may have felt more secure in areas where they lived in larger numbers. For whatever reasons, Knoxville's black population became more densely concentrated in the older wards that made up the pre-1917 city. Those whites who could fled the area, abandoning deteriorating neighborhoods that rapidly were becoming black enclaves.

One observer connected with the recently created TVA noted in the early 1930s that "although the effects are probably not yet apparent, the more rapid increase of negro population [in the old wards of the city] will undoubtedly have some bearing on problems of crime control, housing, provision of educational facilities, etc." Blacks did filter into low-paying, menial jobs, with 92.2 percent of black working females and 29.8 percent of black working males employed as domestics or servants. By 1925 population density for blacks was four times that for whites, and by 1930 property values in five of the nine old city wards had slipped badly (while only four of the city's remaining seventeen wards experienced declines in property values).[54]

As the TVA observer predicted, declining economic status, geographic segregation in deteriorating neighborhoods, and in-migrating rural blacks' problems of adjustment to their new urban environment (social and psychological problems that disturbed many who examined Negro migration) had predictably created breeding grounds for social ills. By 1930 black families without a gainfully employed head of household outnumbered by over three to one families in which the head of household was employed. Over half the black families who paid rent in 1930 were behind in their payments. More serious for the future was the educational mortality rate of the city's young black population. Of those blacks who would have graduated from high school in 1934, only 14.7 percent actually did so—and only approximately one-third (34.0 percent) of the theoretical group had completed more than the fifth grade.[55]

Thus the 1920s witnessed a rapid alteration of Knoxville's traditional demographic patterns, accelerating trends observable earlier. In turn, this change created economic and social problems that would plague the troubled city for years to come. And, for blacks, the problems would be particularly severe.

It would be a mistake, however, to assume that only Knoxville's blacks failed to share in the much-ballyhooed but terribly uneven prosperity of the

[54]TVA Report on Population of Knoxville (unpublished, TVA Technical Library, 1934).

[55]Real Estate Assessment by Wards from Tax Books of County Assessor by TVA, 1934 (copy in TVA Technical Library). For employment statistics see *Fifteenth Census, Population*, IV, 1512, 1533–35. On population density see T.J. Woofter, *Negro Problems in Cities: A Study* (New York, 1928), 79.

A grocery store for white mill workers, Euclid Avenue

MCCLUNG HISTORICAL COLLECTION
KNOXVILLE–KNOX COUNTY PUBLIC LIBRARY

1920s. Working-class whites also suffered the mixed blessings of New South industrialism. In 1930 over 46 percent of the native white male population were employed in manufacturing and mechanical industries, often for pitifully low wages; had no job security; and were fighting to move out of the older wards. Periodic unemployment characterized these industries, and in many families both husbands and wives had to work to make ends meet in the rapidly inflating economy of the 1920s.[56]

Instead of understanding the larger dimensions of their problems, many whites who either could not or would not flee the city vented their frustration and rage against blacks. In their behavior, Knoxville's white working classes mirrored that of many southern whites who were blinded by color to the commonalities of economic interests between whites and blacks. In the early 1920s the Ku Klux Klan had revived as a potent force in the former Confederate states and even had spread into northern and midwestern areas to which blacks had migrated after World War I. In Knoxville a large Klavern of the Invisible Empire was founded, composed mostly of men living or working in close proximity to blacks. Membership records of the Knoxville Klavern indicate that most Klansmen lived in wards Eleven, Fourteen, Fifteen, Sixteen, Seventeen, Eighteen, and Nineteen—an area that roughly ringed the pre-1917 city. Blacks in some numbers had moved into this area, for it was close to the Southern Railway and Coster shops, where many blacks worked. A plurality (26 percent) of those Klansmen who listed their addresses as Knoxville also worked for the Southern Railway, usually at jobs that brought them into direct contact with blacks. For many whites, those blacks became the most visible symbols of their own failure to prosper in the city, of their own dilemma of merging Appalachian traditions and mores with an enforced urban lifestyle, of their own suspicions of their "betters," and of their political impotence.[57]

By the fall of 1923 over two thousand white men had joined the Knoxville Klavern. They attended regular Monday night meetings in a building at the corner of King and West Fourth, traveled to nearby Sharp's Ridge for formal initiations and cross burnings, and generally tried to influence political and business leaders. In the local elections of 1923 the Klan stationed people at all polling places, presumably to influence white voters and discourage Negroes from casting ballots.[58]

But the hysteria that the Ku Klux Klan tried to whip up in Knoxville did not last. Although it expanded its attacks to include the "loose morals" of

[56]*Fifteenth Census* (1930), *Population*, 4: 1512.

[57]The Knoxville Klavern records (including membership records) are in the Knox County Klan Number 14 Papers, Emory University, Atlanta. The above statements come from an analysis of membership records, which contain names, addresses, occupations, religions, ages, number of years in county.

[58]Ibid. See also *Knoxville Journal*, Sept. 23, 1923.

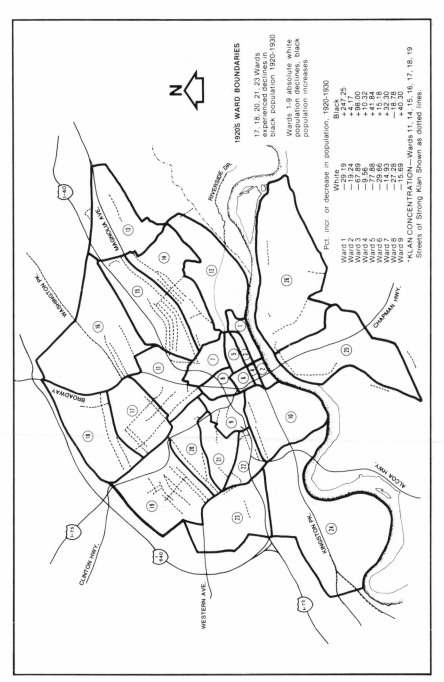

1920S WARD BOUNDARIES

17, 18, 20, 21, 23 Wards
experienced declines in
black population 1920-1930

Wards 1-9 absolute white
population declines, black
population increases

Pct. incr. or decrease in population, 1920-1930

	White	Black
Ward 1	−29.19	+247.25
Ward 2	−19.24	+4.17
Ward 3	−67.89	+98.00
Ward 4	−9.56	+10.32
Ward 5	−77.88	+41.84
Ward 6	−29.66	+15.18
Ward 7	−14.93	+32.30
Ward 8	−27.28	−18.78
Ward 9	−15.69	+40.30

*KLAN CONCENTRATION—Wards 11, 14, 15, 16, 17, 18, 19
Streets of Strong Klan Shown as dotted lines.

1. Ward Boundaries and Ku Klux Klan Concentration, 1920s

the community ("petting parties" and "wild dancing"), the Klan's membership began to decline until by 1928 the local Klavern numbered but 191. The
decline brought a stinging rebuke from the Imperial Palace in Atlanta, but
even the lowering of the initiation fee to $5.00 and then to $3.00 did not halt
the erosion of the KKK in Knoxville.[59]

The decline of the Klan, however, should not be taken as an indication
that the white community had become more tolerant of blacks. Instead, the
white exodus that accelerated during the 1920s very likely robbed the local
Klavern of actual and potential members. The Klan's great gathering at
Chilhowee Park in 1923 marked the high point of local Klan activity, but
certainly not of racial hostility or unrest. On the contrary, Knoxville's blacks
continued to live in a precarious world, with insecure jobs, low wages, and
white suspicion only their greatest challenges.

At the same time that Knoxville's older wards were changing in racial
composition and becoming lower-class enclaves, upper-and upper-middle-
class whites were fleeing westward, beginning one of the most significant
migrations in the region's history. Wards Twenty-four and Twenty-five
(Sequoyah and Talahi, new model planned developments) experienced fan-
tastic population increases of 161.55 percent and 106.69 percent, respectively, between 1920 and 1930, and real estate assessment values in the
former ward almost trebled during the 1920s, going from $2,111,800 in 1920
to an astounding $6,058,950 in 1930. This decade saw one of the great
building booms in the Sequoyah and Cherokee regions, as the business elite,
offended by the noxious odors of the older wards and by their lower-class
populations—white as well as black—moved westward to the lovely new
enclaves being established in West Knoxville.

One might wonder why the University of Tennessee (UT) in the 1920s
seemed so loathe to take an active part in modernizing Knoxville. In fact, the
university appears to have exerted no force at all in community life. Under
President Philander P. Claxton, the university finally (in 1909) had won
annual appropriations from the state legislature, a move that improved the
institution's ability to anticipate budgets and plan for growth. But Claxton's
successor, Harcourt A. Morgan, believed that, in return for this recently
won gain, the university community had to conform to regional mores rather
than try to change them. With a background in agriculture and extension
work, Morgan saw the university's primary role as providing technical
services to the surrounding populace—certainly not as threatening relation-
ships with the legislature or the people by standing at the forefront of
economic or social change. Hence Morgan stood silent when the state
legislature, awash with anti-Darwinian fundamentalism, passed an anti-

[59]K. Ramsey to C.B. Lee, May 12, 1930, in Klan Papers, Emory University. See also
Kenneth T. Jackson, *The Ku Klux Klan in the City, 1915–1930* (New York, 1967), 59–65.

Harcourt A. Morgan

UNIVERSITY OF TENNESSEE PHOTOGRAPHIC SERVICES

evolution law in 1925. Indeed, even before the law was passed, Morgan had condoned the dismissal of some professors who had defied regional opinion and taught Darwinian evolution. When the anti-evolution law did pass, Vanderbilt University faculty member Edwin Mims tried to unite the colleges of Tennessee in protest, but Morgan would not hear of it. Some say the rebuff exacerbated the growing hostility between the two schools. While he might have opposed the law privately, Morgan feared that retribution by the legislature and the populace would damage the university's standing in the community and hamper it in fulfilling its role. When national attention focused on nearby Dayton during the famous Scopes trial of 1925, the university, tightly controlled by Morgan, remained timorously out of the limelight.[60]

Morgan's determination to avoid giving the appearance that UT was out of step with local mores was well illustrated in the 1923 dismissal of law professor John R. Neal. Neal, who had been at the university full time since 1917, was a minor political figure and well-known eccentric who had protested the firing of a professor of education who supposedly had taught evolution. Moreover, Neal had become an administration gadfly who, according to Philip M. Hamer, led an ill-starred campaign for faculty control over appointments and dismissals and took the students' side in almost every university controversy. Finally it was determined that Neal had to go. For his part, Morgan recommended dismissal to the board of trustees, conducted a one-sided hearing into the matter, and later influenced the board to uphold his decision. Two years later, the university "announced that it would no longer give an annual John R. Neal Oratorical Award to the best debate student." Again Morgan had won, and the university remained a timid, conforming force in Knoxville's life—in essence, no force at all.[61]

In sum, then, the cultural fragmentation so typical of New South industrial towns, which was well advanced in Knoxville by 1920, rapidly accelerated in the following decade. Economically, socially, and politically, the city was divided into mutually hostile and suspicious camps of the conservative business elite, Appalachian whites, blacks, insulated university faculty, and a comparatively small middle class. From Talahi mansions to shotgun houses, from Chopin to the recently founded "Grand Ole Opry," from opulent offices to railway shops, from illegally imported scotch whiskey to

[60]On general atmosphere see Bobby Eugene Hicks, "The Great Objector: The Life and Public Career of Dr. John R. Neal," East Tennessee Historical Society *Publications* 41 (1969): 33–66; James R. Montgomery, "John R. Neal and the University of Tennessee: A Five-Part Tragedy," *Tennessee Historical Quarterly* 37 (Summer 1979): 214–34; Ray Ginger, *Six Days or Forever? Tennessee v. John Thomas Scopes* (Boston, 1958), 79, 212.

[61]John William Routh, "The John R. Neal Law School" (unpublished [1979], being prepared for publication; draft in College Scholars Office, Univ. of Tennessee). Montgomery, "John R. Neal," 228–33.

potent moonshine, the fissures in what had once been a comparatively homogeneous community by 1930 had widened until few men or women could bridge the gaps. At the onset of the Great Depression, Knoxville was a city fragmented along class and race lines; suspicions of change and of each other were its citizens' only common denominators.

THE GREAT DEPRESSION

Neither elite nor workers were prepared to comprehend or deal with the Great Depression that swept over the land in the early 1930s. Symptomatic of its effect on Knoxville was the almost universal failure of the city's banking community. During the 1920s local banks had been pressed by their stockholders to pay liberal dividends, a policy that in the short run had been profitable to investors but ultimately proved shortsighted. Caught by the stock market crash with insufficient capital, with too many large loans to personal friends and stockholders, and with a too liberal dividend policy, Knoxville banks fell like dominoes before the onslaught of the national crisis. Again the city's elite, eager to take short-run profits rather than wait for long-term investments to pay off, proved hopelessly shortsighted and unimaginative.[62]

In 1930 the Guaranty Trust Company went into receivership, along with the largest real estate firm in the city. When the Bank of Tennessee (wholly owned by the Caldwell and Company Investment House) went into receivership in November, the reverberations spread to Knoxville's major bank (in which Caldwell had invested heavily), the Holston-Union. On November 10, 1930, a run on that institution resulted in $750,000 in withdrawals and, despite a Federal Reserve loan, the Holston-Union closed its doors on Armistice Day. From there the panic spread. In an effort to merge several weakened banks into one strong one, the East Tennessee National, East Tennessee Savings, and the City National reformed themselves as the East Tennessee National Bank. But in spite of loans from the Federal Reserve and President Hoover's Reconstruction Finance Corporation, the new East Tennessee National collapsed in January 1932. By 1932, of the six national banks in Knoxville in 1920, three had disappeared through merger and three more had been forced into receivership. Drained by shortsighted stockholders, by poor banking practices, and ultimately by loss of public confidence, Knoxville's banks simply could not withstand the strains of the Great Depression. Some depositors escaped with their savings, but many more were wiped out by their banks' failures.[63]

[62]White, "Banking Developments," in Deaderick, ed., *Heart of the Valley*, 377–78.
[63]Ibid., 387–88.

As the national economy lurched downward, the city felt the full force of the Depression's fury. Construction virtually stopped, with building permits plummeting from 2,207 in 1928 to 1,246 in 1929 and on to a disastrous 757 in 1930. Telephones were disconnected, memberships in civic clubs dropped alarmingly, and bread lines and soup kitchens began to appear on once-bustling Gay Street and at the General Hospital. More serious, the city's population increase during the 1930s was a paltry 5.5 percent (from 105,797 in 1930 to 111,580 in 1940), a clear sign that many people were abandoning Knoxville, either quixotically to seek employment in other cities or to retrace their once-hopeful steps back to the hills and hollows of the surrounding hinterland.[64]

As the Depression deepened, Knoxville's employment picture became exceedingly bleak. With the city dependent on low-grade manufacturing and mechanical industries, factory closings threw a high proportion of the labor force out of work. Unemployment statistics crept disturbingly upward, from 2,284 unemployed in 1930 to 7,534 in 1937. By March 1939, in spite of President Franklin Roosevelt's ambitious-sounding New Deal, over 6,000 Knox Countians were still on relief. By 1940 the picture had barely brightened, with 4,332 city residents still seeking work; 1,703 employed by Work Projects Administration (WPA) projects, and over 1,500 working for the TVA.

The economic catastrophe had important effects on Knoxville. With wages of those who could find jobs badly deflated, a decline in the standard of living was almost inevitable. Nonunion wages for carpenters were 65¢ per hour, truck drivers 40¢ per hour, common laborers 30¢ per hour, and textile workers (of whom there were approximately 6,000) about 35¢ per hour. Unemployment and frustration took their toll on the working-class citizens, who poured out their wrath upon one another. In 1938, for the first time in the city's checkered history, homicide was among the ten leading causes of death for Knoxvillians.[65]

With banks destroyed and public revenue rapidly drying up, Knoxville's local government staggered into the Depression with an enormous bonded

[64]On building permits see "Building Permits in Knoxville, 1923–1933" (unpub. TVA report, 1934, TVA Technical Library), table 11A. The number of houses built between 1930 and 1934 was but 823, one-third the number of homes constructed during the preceding five-year period. On telephone disconnections see "Telephone Facilities and Services, Knoxville, 1924–1934," data furnished to TVA by E.F. Garratt, District Manager of the Southern Bell Telephone Company (TVA Technical Library). On civic clubs see "Membership of Selected Social and Civic Clubs, Knoxville" (TVA report, 1934). Knox County civic clubs experienced a similar decline in membership. See ibid. Though the births and deaths per 1,000 population were lowest for Knoxville of any large city in the state, the low growth rate of population clearly points to significant out-migration, both to the county and beyond.

[65]All figures are for Mar. 1939, from *Commercial and Industrial Survey of Knoxville, Tennessee*, for the Chamber of Commerce (Knoxville, 1939).

indebtedness. Forced to the brink of financial ruin, the municipality was obliged to pay its employees in scrip and had to refund its public debt to 1978. Since Knoxvillians were defaulting on their city taxes in droves, the harried city council had no alternative but to beg for mercy from its creditors and simultaneously to issue more bonds.[66]

The Depression also created a semi-transient population in Knoxville, men and women who floated in and out of the troubled city as well as from house to house or apartment to apartment. Though homeowners appear to have been a rock of stability in the city (with but 5.4 percent of them having moved during the year 1939), lower middle-class and lower-class renters seem to have been constantly moving about, entering the city in search of employment and leaving soon afterward, disappointed, only to be replaced by a new influx of desperate job seekers. In 1939 fully 38.4 percent of the city's renters had lived in their houses or apartments less than eleven months. Thus, below the comparatively stable middle class, Knoxville was constantly in flux, and its people were continually disoriented.[67]

Knoxville's housing had deteriorated badly before the Depression, and economic hard times made it nearly impossible to make needed improvements. A 1934 Department of Commerce real property survey ranked Knoxville "low" among sixty-four cities surveyed, with 24.3 percent of its 22,828 residential structures in "bad" condition, 28 percent "too crowded," 40 percent lacking bathtubs or showers, and 21.9 percent having three rooms or less (the famous "shotgun" house). Federal aid to a new municipal housing authority constituted an attempt to alleviate the housing problem, but it was some time before the effects of this were either felt or seen.[68]

Knoxville's blacks were hit especially hard by the national catastrophe. Whites fleeing from foreclosed farms or lost urban jobs demanded and generally received employment, as blacks were bumped off payrolls in alarming numbers.[69] Whereas in 1924 practically all the city's asphalt and paving workers had been black, a decade later only four or five Negroes had been able to maintain those politically sensitive positions. By 1934 the telephone company, which had employed blacks even to the foreman level,

[66]Lyndon E. Abbott and Lee S. Greene, *Municipal Government and Administration in Tennessee*, no. 5 of the School of Business Administration Bureau of Research, Univ. of Tennessee (Knoxville, 1939), 113.

[67]Ibid., 29; *Commercial and Industrial Survey of Knoxville, Tennessee* (1939).

[68]Abbott and Greene, *Municipal Government*, 29. Of the dwellings considered residential structures, 12.4% were more than 40 years old in 1934. Of 25,851 dwelling units, nearly 30% were classed as "too crowded." Nearly 40% of the dwelling units rented for under $15 per month and one-fourth were without gas or electricity.

[69]For a survey of whites fleeing or being removed from the area's rural regions see Michael J. McDonald, "Appalachian Stereotypes and Quality of Life Variance: TVA's Norris Dam Population Removal Problems" (unpub. paper presented to the Southern Regional Science Association, Apr. 1976).

reported no black employees. Similar cases can be cited in other vocations and trades: the city's baking trade, formerly all black, was by 1934 all white; chefs and cooks in 1929 were all black, but by 1934 there were only two Negro cooks in the city; railroads, once primary employers of blacks, during the Depression simply stopped hiring them; not only the carpentry and masonry trades, but also marble and quarry work saw declines, black employment in the latter dropping by 66 percent; and over 75 percent of even the normally black janitors and porters were replaced by whites. The economic suffering of whites was mitigated by their wholesale displacement of black workers.[70]

Nor did the vaunted New Deal cushion blacks' hardships in the reeling city. In 1934 not one black laborer was listed on the payrolls of the Civil Works Authority, a fact that led some to protest that the CWA was consciously discriminating against Negro job seekers. The blue eagle of the National Recovery Administration (NRA) did not benefit black workers, either; in fact, because NRA codes stipulated minimum wage rates, many employers chose to fire their black workers rather than pay them the code-imposed wages. So, in some cases the NRA brought reverses for the Negro, not recovery. Sensitive as they were to the political and social pulses of the region, the NRA and its parent, the New Deal, had almost no impact on Knoxville blacks.[71]

Blacks also charged that the newly created TVA was "bending over backwards not to give any offense to the traditions of the South." It is hard to say whether the Authority's employment practices concerning blacks was due more to the New Deal's desire to accommodate itself to regional mores or to TVA director Arthur Morgan's personal racial views. Whatever the reason, blacks were excluded from the new TVA-built "model community" of Norris, were hired (when at all) only for the most menial jobs, and then were segregated into separate work crews. Clearly, the national reform movement of the New Deal, for whatever reasons, failed dismally to assist Knoxville's black population, men and women who had considerably more to fear than fear itself.[72]

In addition to bleak economic prospects, Knoxville's Negroes continued to face serious social problems. Unemployed, impotent, and angry, blacks poured out their frustration in acts of violence. Larceny, homicide, and all

[70]Charles S. Johnson, comp., "The Negro Population of the Tennessee Valley Area" (unpub. report by TVA, CWA and Fisk University, 1934, TVA Technical Library), 2: 106–7; Lorin A. Thompson, "Urbanization, Occupational Shift and Economic Progress," in Vance and Demerath, eds., *The Urban South*, 48–49.

[71]Johnson, "The Negro Population of the Tennessee Valley Area," 2: 113.

[72]Charles H. Houston and John P. Davis, "TVA: Lily-White Reconstruction," *The Crisis* 41 (Oct. 1934): 290–91, 311; John P. Davis, "The Plight of the Negro in the Tennessee Valley," *The Crisis* 42 (Oct. 1935): 294–95, 314–15.

types of juvenile delinquency plagued the black community. In 1930, for example, the homicide rate for Negroes was almost six times that for whites. Of all Negroes arrested and convicted of crimes in Knoxville in 1931, almost one-half (48.2 percent) listed "no occupation" on their police records. Over one-half of the black juvenile delinquents came from broken homes; desertion by frustrated males was so common that in 1934 one-third of the black families in the city listed female heads of households. School attendance among black youths decreased drastically, with only about one-third (39.3 percent) remaining in school through the fifth grade. Not surprisingly, in Knoxville Negro illiteracy was nearly three times as great as that of whites. Yet black residences were hardly ideal centers for raising children who had dropped out of school. A TVA-sponsored study showed a disturbingly low standard of living among even the most geographically stable of black families. One example will suffice: 59.2 percent of blacks surveyed by TVA used no electricity, as opposed to 15.4 percent of surveyed whites. Clearly, if the Depression was taking a heavy toll among black adults, its social by-products augured ill for the futures of black adults-to-be in the East Tennessee city.[73]

Some Knoxville blacks chose to abandon the troubled city, as did southern blacks in general, either following rumors of opportunities in the North or retreating to the desperate rural regions from whence they had come. During the 1930s Knoxville witnessed a massive black out-migration, so large that the number of Negroes in the city declined by almost 1,000 persons, from 17,093 in 1930 to 16,106 in 1940. To the blacks of this New South city, the promise of American life seemed to lie elsewhere, and the New Deal meant only continued accommodation to old ways of white survival at the expense of Negro degradation.[74]

---

[73] The 1930 homicide rate for Negroes was 78 per 100,000 black population as opposed to a white homicide rate of 14 per 100,000 white population. Johnson, "The Negro Population of the Tennessee Valley Area," 1: 148. On high crime rate and juvenile delinquency among the city's blacks see ibid., 1: 168, 2: 88–89. On occupation of blacks arrested and convicted of crimes in Knoxville in 1931 and 1932 see ibid., 1: 164. On percentage of females who were heads of households see ibid., 2: 61. On school attendance and grades completed in 1934 for Knoxville see ibid., 2: 64–70. Knoxville public schools for blacks had only eleven grades. Ibid., 1: 16. Illiteracy in Knoxville for blacks was nearly three times that for whites. Ibid., 1:16. On low standard of living for the city's blacks see William J. Durbin, "Household Equipment Survey, Knoxville, Tennessee 1934" (unpub. TVA-CWA Project 76B, TVA Technical Library). Durbin surveyed 13,505 Knoxvillians (2,296 of whom were black). Also on standard of living and employment, in 1934 Johnson sampled 101 families in Ward 5, an area with a heavy concentration (94.99% in 1930) of blacks. See Johnson, "The Negro Population of the Tennessee Valley Area," 1: 177.

[74] Between 1930 and 1940 black population in Knoxville declined from 17,093 to 16,106, a net loss of 987. Taking natural increase into account, the out-migration would be significant indeed.

Perhaps the Depression's greatest impact on Knoxville, and one that no government could adequately assuage, was on the city's collective mentality. Caroline Bird has called the Great Depression an "invisible scar,"[75] a psychological wound that would irrevocably separate those who lived through it from those who did not. In Knoxville the scars of deprivation were slow to heal. The optimistic booster spirit of an earlier epoch was mortally wounded, leaving a legacy of rigid conservatism and defensiveness as shrill as it was unconvincing. True, these attitudes had always been present in the city, at least since the Civil War. But the Great Depression acted to deepen these intellectual gullies and make it difficult for anything to hold out against the onrushing tide. In Knoxville the legacy included a suspicion of change and innovation; a desperate clinging to the eternal verities of family, church, prohibition, and making ends meet; deep lines of demarcation between economic, social, and racial groups; and a fanatical defense of the city itself against the criticisms of "outsiders," whether they represented TVA, the university, or some other group. The dreams of the New South advocates of so long ago had all come true. But for some, those dreams of industrialism and urbanization had turned to nightmares.

[75] Caroline Bird, *The Invisible Scar* (New York, 1966).

IN THE MID-1940s, well-known traveler-writer John Gunther briefly visited Knoxville, gathering material for his next book, planned as a sequel to the enormously popular *Inside Europe* (1936), *Inside Asia* (1939), and *Inside Latin America* (1941). The eventual result, *Inside U.S.A.* (1946), was a curious mixture of praise, criticism, and impressionistic reporting of what Gunther himself (in typical "Gunther-ese") called "the greatest, craziest, most dangerous, least stable, most spectacular, least grown-up, and most powerful and magnificent nation ever known."[1]

Though brief, Gunther's time in Knoxville must have been less than pleasant, for the author penned one of the most scathing attacks on the city ever printed—one so critical, in fact, that as late as the 1970s his name alone could bring forth expletives that many Knoxvillians usually reserved for Democrats or the unchurched. Gunther wrote,

> Knoxville is the ugliest city I ever saw in America, with the possible exception of some mill towns in New England. Its main street is called Gay Street; this seemed to me to be a misnomer. A recent movie, "Ziegfield Follies of 1946," could only be shown in a cut version in Knoxville, because one sequence shows Lena Horne. Knoxville, an extremely puritanical town, serves no alcohol stronger than 3.6 percent beer, and its most dignified taprooms close at 9:30 p.m.; Sunday movies are forbidden, and there is no Sunday baseball. Perhaps as a result, it is one of the least orderly cities in the South—Knoxville leads every other town in Tennessee in homicides, automobile thefts, and larceny.[2]

Were that not enough, in his conclusion Gunther remarked that the city possessed "an intense, concentrated, degrading ugliness."[3]

The reaction of most Knoxvillians to Gunther's assault was predictable. Years later, some remembered that the author's comments elicited more

---

[1]John Gunther, *Inside U.S.A.* (New York, 1946), xvi.
[2]Ibid., 761.
[3]Ibid., 910.

*Church Street Viaduct in the 1920s,
looking toward the site of the present Civic Coliseum (on right)*

BECK CULTURAL EXCHANGE CENTER

unity (against Gunther) than almost any issue before or since. Sidewalk interviews by the Knoxville *News-Sentinel* also revealed unanimous hostility. And for its part, the Knoxville *Journal* refused to print one word about Gunther's remarks, preferring instead to agonize over the communist influence in Hollywood or to defend syndicated columnist and New Deal archenemy Westbrook Pegler.[4]

Perhaps the most interesting and perceptive reaction to Gunther's diatribe came from Knoxville journalist Lucy Templeton, whose *News-Sentinel* column "A Country Calendar" was a chatty, popular mixture of history, book notes, recipes, and local color. In her column of June 1, 1946, Templeton stung fellow Knoxvillians by admitting that Gunther had been basically correct and that the city she loved was a grimy, sooty, ugly place despite its location amidst the natural beauty of the Smoky Mountains. Worse, she questioned whether Knoxvillians even possessed the will to recognize their problems, face up to them, and solve them. Readers may have seethed, but Templeton, a Bryn Mawr alumna and a 1901 UT graduate, charter member of the Pi chapter of Chi Omega sorority, widow of George Mabry Templeton (a prominent Knoxvillian and local attorney), and *Sentinel* staffer off and on from 1904, was so impeccably connected that no one dared publicly to rebuke her.[5]

While the vast majority of Knoxvillians would not have admitted it, almost certainly Lucy Templeton was more accurate in her portrayal of the city's physical and psychological landscape than those who blustered against the best-selling Gunther. What even Templeton had failed to see, however, was precisely why Knoxville had been unable in the 1940s to marshal its not-inconsiderable assets to move the city into the postwar economic boom and to attack its most glaring physical, political, and psychological problems. And while the debate over John Gunther raged, modestly positive economic indicators were masking the central problem that would sap Knoxville both economically and psychologically for years to come—the continuing demographic deterioration of the city.

WAR AND POSTWAR BOOMLET

The war and postwar years witnessed a dramatic rejuvenation of the American economy, which eradicated all but the deepest memories of the Great Depression. The nation's gross national product, already stimulated by wartime production, continued its impressive ascent after the war, rising

[4]Smart Club Address, Nov. 25, 1980; *Journal*, June–Aug. 1946; *News-Sentinel*, June 1, 1946.

[5]*News-Sentinel*, June 1, 1946. On Lucy Templeton see Deaderick, ed., *Heart of the Valley*, 612–13.

from $283 billion in 1946 to $367 billion in 1953. During the postwar era, unemployment was almost eradicated or at least hit an almost irreducible minimum; disposable personal income increased markedly; and, in spite of postwar inflation, Americans in general experienced one of the most prosperous periods in their history. Indeed, except for the nation's farmers, almost every sector of the national economy seemed to thrive, with automobiles, chemicals (including synthetics), electronics, new metals and fuels, and aviation leading the way. Even the South, usually the poor stepchild of the industrial era, increased its share of U.S. manufacturing and prospered.[6]

On the surface Knoxville appeared to participate in these beneficial national trends. Almost indigestible amounts of federal government money had been funneled into the city during the war, principally to the firms of Rohm and Haas (which made plexiglass for airplanes) and the Aluminum Company of America (ALCOA), Oak Ridge (where the major part of the Manhattan Project was carried out in a brand-new town that eventually contained 75,000 people); the TVA (which constructed dams at nearby Douglas, Cherokee, and Fontana lakes) also attracted enormous federal monies. And in the postwar years federal money continued to pour into the city through these institutions, though certainly not on the grand scale of the war years.[7]

Banking in Knoxville seemed to mirror the new prosperity. From slightly over $61 million in 1940, assets grew to nearly $210 million in 1945, with the Hamilton National Bank holding over half of the city's total assets. And while the end of the war brought a $32-million decrease in bank resources as the federal government reduced both its local bank deposits and debt obligations, the unexpected rapid shift to peacetime productivity showed the banking establishments' vitality, as loans and discounts increased by $12,000,000, or 59 percent. Knoxville's banks appear to have been in a good position to aid the city both in wartime and in postwar recovery.[8]

Other signs also seemed to indicate that the city would participate in the postwar prosperity. The construction industry, a key employer in the re-

[6] Arthur S. Link and William B. Catton, *The Era of the Cold War, 1946–1973*, vol. 3 of *American Epoch: A History of the United States Since 1900* 4th ed. (New York, 1974), 1–28 and passim.

[7] For a general study of TVA's wartime development and its contributions to the war effort, see Don McBride, "TVA and National Defense" (Knoxville, TVA, 1975, unpub. manuscript). On the impact of Oak Ridge, see William E. Cole, "Urban Development in the Tennessee Valley," *Social Forces* 26 (Oct. 1947): 68; and Charles W. Johnson and Charles O. Jackson, *City Behind a Fence: Oak Ridge, Tennessee, 1942–1946* (Knoxville, 1981).

[8] Deaderick, ed., *Heart of the Valley*, 292–93 and table 9. For a fuller discussion of wartime and postwar banking impacts in Knoxville see ibid., 393–96, and table 10.

gion, had been artificially stimulated during the war by the building of Oak Ridge and, in the late 1940s, continued to prosper as building permit values soared from an anemic $2,518,728 in 1940 to over $12 million in 1946, leveling off at a still impressive $10,290,747 in 1947. Too, Knoxvillians' dramatically increased buying power (in 1943 the city's effective per capita buying income was $268 higher than the national average and more than twice that of Tennessee as a whole) spurred expansion of retail, wholesale, and service jobs; employment in those areas doubled in the 1940s. In 1943 the city's total effective buying power had increased by 134.68 percent over that of 1938 and, despite postwar inflation, in the late 1940s continued to rise. Pent-up demand for consumer goods made its impact felt at the war's end. In 1946 retail sales for the county and city were $143,366,000, of which the city's share was $134,253,000. The rest of the decade saw continued growth. In 1950 retail sales were $204,262,000, of which the city's share was $184,487,000. The city's portion of this retail trade would remain strong in the years ahead, although it should be noted that in the 1940s the county's portion had increased dramatically.[9]

The general postwar prosperity also seemed to have infected Knoxville's civic leaders, for they began to make great plans for urban rejuvenation and beautification. The Knoxville Housing Authority (KHA) was organized as a tax-exempt public corporation in 1936, though it took a series of court decisions (the final one being handed down from the Tennessee Supreme Court) to uphold its status and power. Immediately, the KHA undertook a survey of the city's housing stock with an eye to reform. By 1949 the survey, "a study of Knoxville's blighted areas," was completed and plans for urban redevelopment produced. This at last was a vital step in the city's development, for as one observer later noted, "Expressway construction was coordinated, to a degree, with redevelopment. The two activities together resulted in radical alterations in Knoxville's appearance, its population, and the functions of its urban systems."[10]

Further signs of modernism were seen with the opening of the Knoxville Airport in 1937, and the city's request two years later that the Knoxville Transit Lines (KTL) convert trolley cars to buses on its routes. This latter request was a sure sign that civic leaders expected growth beyond the existing trolley tracks, and although the switch to buses did not actually take place until 1947, at least the plans had been made and carried out with what was, for Knoxville, uncharacteristic dispatch.[11]

[9]In 1943 Knoxville ranked 89th of 132 U.S. cities over 100,000 population in buying income per capita. Comparably sized cities with less buying power than Knoxville were Chattanooga; Reading, Pa.; Miami, Fla.; and Savannah, Ga.

[10]Deaderick, ed., *Heart of the Valley*, 120.

[11]Ibid., 230.

Concomitantly, in 1938 the City of Knoxville took possession of its electric power system, after a six-year struggle to convert to public power. In 1939 the Electric Power and Water Board became forerunner of the present Knoxville Utilities Board (KUB). As has been mentioned, TVA's wartime construction work on the Fontana, Cherokee, Douglas, and Fort Loudon dams stimulated the local economy. Fort Loudon Dam, built just above the point where the Little Tennssee River joins the Tennessee, was the dam closest to Knoxville on the main river systems. Building it meant that TVA's nine-foot navigable channel would extend behind the locks to Knoxville, thus altering the city's riverfront considerably. This spurred the city planning commission to employ Harlan Bartholomew Associates to develop a plan for Knoxville's riverfront, potentially a beautiful area but one that in fact was badly scarred by slums and haphazard industrial siting. The riverfront plan, adopted in 1941, recommended construction of a series of riverfront parks along a projected highway from Concord Street to Riverside Drive (today's Neyland Drive). The plan, in effect, mapped out a complete facelift for a city badly in need of one.[12]

Material improvements, organizational developments, and plans encompassing public power, public housing authority, transportation reforms, and a new airport, coupled with the economic harvest of the wartime years, appeared to have left Knoxville poised on the brink of a new era of development. Superficially, at least, there seemed every reason to believe that Knoxville had overcome the municipal financial woes of the previous era as well as the economic blows of the Depression and that the city was fully launched into the postwar urbanization so characteristic of many southern cities. But beneath these promising signs there lay a different reality.

POSTWAR PROBLEMS

Reflecting on the preliminary results of the 1950 United States census, the Knoxville *News-Sentinel* sounded the first note of warning that all was not well. In an article titled "Outskirts call youngsters, but Ma, Pa, stay put," the local afternoon newspaper began to analyze what others would later recognize as the demographic devitalization of the city itself. Although the *News-Sentinel*'s piece was superficial, nevertheless it was the first observation that Knoxville in the 1940s had failed to hold the young and the economically advantaged and that an increasing proportion of those remaining in the city were older and poorer citizens. This trend was part of a national one, soon to be dubbed "suburbanization," which left many American cities—

12Ibid., 118.

including Knoxville—with growing problems and momentous decisions.[13]

Knoxville and Knox County did not share evenly in the 1940s population growth. While the county, excluding the city, grew 45.1 percent between 1940 and 1950, the city increased a meager 11.8 percent. The city's increase was particularly small in view of the fact that 5,100 UT students, not categorized as city residents in 1940, were counted as Knoxvillians in the 1950 census. Without the addition of those students, the city's population growth would have been about 7 percent, not even enough to match the city's natural increase.[14]

To be sure, this trend was also to be observed during the depression-stricken 1930s. But in that decade it had always been assumed—probably correctly—that people were leaving the city because of the paucity of job opportunities. How, then, could one explain the continuation of this out-migration in the supposedly prosperous wartime and postwar decade of the 1940s? More to the point, how could anyone deny the fact that Knoxville would soon face serious problems, when, since 1930, all of the six civil districts in the metropolitan area contiguous to the city had been growing faster than the city itself? Indeed, thoughtful readers of the *News-Sentinel* article of October 1, 1950, had good cause for concern.[15]

Two explanations can be offered for Knoxville's seeming inability to participate in the relatively widespread postwar boom. After the war the textile industry, the city's biggest industrial employer, went into decline. Changing markets and transportation networks, new product development, and new technologies combined to make Knoxville's older industries less competitive in the midst of a general slump in textiles. With its older and basic industrial base slowed down, the city's general industrial employment growth was not fast enough to continue to absorb new people from the hinterlands. In addition, as will be explained more fully in chapter 3, Knoxville was in the process of shifting to a greater orientation toward the service

[13]*News-Sentinel*, Oct. 1, 1950. For an interesting discussion of these trends nationally, see Howard P. Chudacoff, *The Evolution of American Urban Society* 2nd ed. (Englewood Cliffs, N.J., 1981), 264–67.

[14]Hammer and Company Associates, "The Economy of Metropolitan Knoxville," prepared for the Metropolitan Planning Commission of Knoxville and Knox County (Washington, D.C., 1962), 76. Cited hereafter as the Hammer report.

[15]For a detailed analysis of Knoxville's population growth in the years 1940–1950 (metro, city, and Knox County) see Hammer report, 59–78. As early as the 1930s the fastest growing segments of Knoxville's population were in civil districts contiguous to the city limits proper, which if containing 150 persons per square mile were classed as "metropolitan" Knoxville. These were in the northeast and the west, districts two and eight, respectively. Knoxville *News-Sentinel*, Mar. 13, 1941. For every person added to Knoxville's population from the inner city, two were added from the suburban fringes of the metropolitan districts outside the city. Cole, "Urban Development," 70.

sector of the economy. The Knoxville *Journal* noted sadly that between 1940 and 1950 industrial employment within the city had increased only 9 percent, and that this formerly great component of the city's economic and population growth was moribund. Naturally, without a significant increase in job opportunities, it would be folly to expect young and middle-aged workers to remain in the city when better opportunities existed elsewhere. And many did leave, prompting the *News-Sentinel* to worry over the city's economic future. The city planning engineers were troubled, noting that between "1880 and 1920 Knoxville grew more steadily than the nation. Since then the city has declined steadily and as of 1950 only 56 percent of the [county's] population lives within city limits. The most favorable growth opportunities are past."[16]

Lack of employment opportunities was a serious but correctible problem. Knoxville's other serious problem (the one identified by Gunther and Templeton), however, was more complex. Since World War I, the city's core had grown progressively less attractive, covered by a thin layer of coal dust. Housing stock in the core had deteriorated badly, and after World War II the rejuvenated construction industry preferred to invest in suburban development rather than core renewal. And the city itself lacked the funds to carry out core beautification and riverfront improvement plans. As Edith Howard of the Tennessee Bureau of Public Administration noted acidly in her study of the municipal waterfronts of the state: "To date [1949] the city's financial condition has precluded any start towards physical development, estimated to cost over $5,000,000. More disheartening than the lack of improvements is the evidence pointing to laxity in following the waterfront plan as originally adopted. Land originally dedicated for park purposes furnished the site on which a hospital was constructed." Hence, though Gunther in the mid-1940s failed to understand Knoxville's deep troubles, he did see a city that was hardly pretty.[17]

Perhaps the KHA survey of Knoxville's housing stock in 1939 identified the most disturbing part of the picture and the most difficult to correct. Over 40 percent of the city's 23,450 dwellings had been built between 1895 and 1914 and were declining rapidly. Mechanicsville and McAnnaly Flats (roughly north of the present I-40 and west of I-75), the post-Civil War working-class neighborhoods housing railroad and iron workers, were "undergoing rapid deterioration . . . within a maze of industrial plants and railroads." There were 1,623 residences in the area, 1,000 of which had been built prior to 1904, and 912 were classed as physically substandard.

[16]*Journal*, Dec. 17, 1950.

[17]Edith Foster Howard, "Riverfront: The Protection of Municipal Waterfronts in Tennessee," *University of Tennessee Record*, Extension Series 25, no. 1 (Knoxville, Mar. 1949), 22.

Throughout the entire city, 43.6 percent of the residences were said to be substandard.[18]

Among the oldest wards (Wards One through Eight), the situation was worse. These eight wards comprised the central business district (retail and wholesale trade, light manufacturing) and with few exceptions were described in 1939 as in a state of rapid deterioration. Some of the areas between Vine Street and Broadway were frankly characterized as slums, and it was noted that this blight was spreading rapidly eastward along Hill Avenue, Riverside Drive, and Mountain View along the river to the city limits. In Ward One, 25 percent of all the dwelling units had been constructed before 1885.[19]

Throughout the city, 20 percent of all houses were classed as in need of major repairs and 24.5 percent as unfit for use; 40 percent were reported to possess less than one toilet and one bath. Of course, as noted above, housing in the core was worse; in Wards Nine, Twenty, Twenty-one, and Twenty-two, over 60 percent of the dwellings lacked one bath and one toilet. And some areas, such as the predominantly black Mountain View (site of the present Downtown Loop, Hyatt Regency, and city police building), continued to deteriorate even more into the 1960s, when U.S. President Lyndon B. Johnson in 1964 identified residents of Mountain View as "people as poverty-ridden as I have seen in any part of the United States."[20]

The 1939 KHA report was primarily concerned with the spreading effects of urban blight, which radiated in concentric circles from an inner-city railroad nexus placed roughly at Broadway and Jackson Avenue and Second Creek. This blight affected even the edges of wards farther out that had vacant usable space and fewer older buildings. The net effect of this spreading blight was to encourage out-migration and contribute to a general physical unattractiveness that discouraged private redevelopment as well as in-migration. In spite of the fact that a WPA-sponsored city property inventory revealed that Knoxville had a great deal of unused land "available for residential utilization [that] will comfortably supply housing room to support a population of 200,000," few chose the city over the newer, cleaner, safer suburban enclaves.[21]

[18]City of Knoxville, Knoxville Housing Authority, "Real Property Inventory and Low Income Housing Area Survey of Knoxville, Tennessee," WPA Project No. 665-44-3-11 (Knoxville, 1939), 19, 21, 23, 24; chart 7, p. 42; block tabulation, Ward 9, p. 60.

[19]Ibid., 23; pt. 3, p. 52.

[20]Ibid., charts 5, 7, and 9, pp. 38, 42, 45. Racial breakdowns were as follows: Ward 1: 20% black, 80% white; Ward 5: 5% white, 95% black; Ward 7: 52% white, 48% black; Ward 9: 68% white, 32% black; Ward 12: 60% white, 40% black; Ward 19: 81% white, 19% black; Ward 21: 52% white, 48% black; Ward 20: 100% white; Ward 22: 92% white, 8% black; and Ward 23: 99% white, 1% black. For Johnson's statement see *News-Sentinel*, May 8, 1964.

[21]Ibid., 19. The City Planning Commission's projected population for 1950 was 200,000

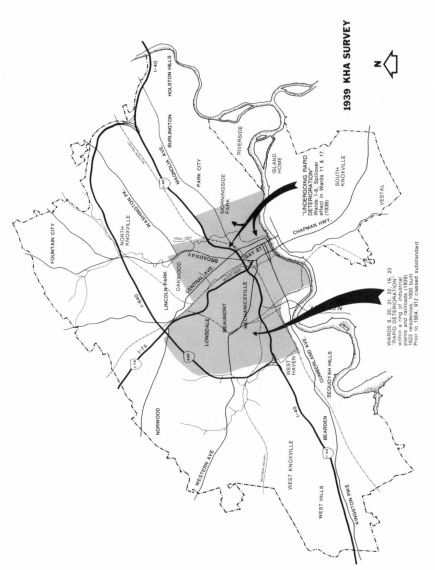

1939 KHA SURVEY

N

HOLSTON HILLS

BURLINGTON

MAGNOLIA AVE.

PARK CITY

RIVERSIDE

MORNINGSIDE PARK

ISLAND HOME

WASHINGTON PKE.

"UNDERGOING RAPID
DETERIORATION"
Wards 1-8, Spillover
effect in Wards 11 & 17.
(1939)

SOUTH KNOXVILLE

VESTAL

NORTH KNOXVILLE

FOUNTAIN CITY

CHAPMAN HWY.

BROADWAY

GAY ST.

LINCOLN PARK

OAKWOOD

CENTRAL AVE.

I-640

MECHANICSVILLE

LONSDALE

BEAUMONT

I-75

I-40

I-76

WEST HAVEN

CUMBERLAND AVE.

SEQUOYAH HILLS

NORWOOD

WESTERN AVE.

WEST KNOXVILLE

BEARDEN

WEST HILLS

KINGSTON PIKE

I-40

WARDS 9, 20, 21, 22, 19, 23
"RAPID DETERIORATION"
within a ring of industrial
plants and railroads (1939)
1623 residences, 1000 built
Prior to 1904, 912 classed substandard

11. Knoxville Housing Authority Survey, 1939

And as the city slowly deteriorated, the vitality of the suburban fringe grew unabated. Between 1940 and 1947 the KUB reported a 231.7 percent increase in county water connections. Suburban development in the north and west was rapid, though not rapid enough to alleviate the postwar housing shortage. In some areas within the city limits, notably Sequoyah and Cherokee Hills, new housing was constructed, mostly filling in vacant areas not developed in the 1920s and 1930s. For the most part, however, suburban development was being carried on beyond the city limits. Within the core, the limits of Knoxville's participation in the postwar prosperity were reflected increasingly in the city's physical landscape.[22]

Gunther and Templeton were not the only ones to observe this phenomenon. David Madden, Knoxville native and UT graduate, used the city as the setting for a novel (*Bijou*, 1976) and a collection of short stories (*The Shadow Knows*, 1963). In the guise of the thirteen-year-old Lucius Hutchfield, Madden guided readers through the Knoxville of the 1940s. Lucius walked down to the riverfront behind the county courthouse, wondering

> where the gospel singing was coming from. Even though they reeked of pee-stained mustiness, stale beer, turnip greens, fried river fish, dirty clothes, dog squat, slop, he was drawn to the old houses. . . . From one porch a pure drop down the cliff into the river . . . down here along the river Negroes and whites more thoroughly mixed than anywhere else in Cherokee [Madden's fictitious name for Knoxville].
>
> A complex network of paths, big rocks, trees, little and scrawny, kudzu vines, made the bluffs behind the houses rugged. Lucius stood on the railroad tracks. He looked back toward the houses. The back yards were full of garbage, trash, crude rabbit hutches, beehives, chicken coops and a few pig pens. The houses looked as though they had been there since the beginning of Cherokee.[23]

To Madden, Knoxville during the 1940s still retained a strong rural flavor and consciousness, even in the heart of the business district. Lucius

> enjoyed passing through the ancient three story, block long, brick market house, its arched ceiling looming over them, a line of rough little tables running down the spine of the building where country

---

persons. Even in 1970, however, after the massive annexations of 1962, the city was still 25,000 persons short of that projection.

[22] Cole, "Urban Development," 68. In 1947 persons per water connection were between 5.5 and 6, compared with a 1940 figure of 4.7. Such was the filling in and crowding of the core that many single-family dwellings had been converted to hold two or more families.

[23] David Madden, *Bijou* (New York, 1976), 63–64. Many had been there that long. Of the dwelling units in Ward 1 (banked by Gay Street, the river eastward to Ferry, and in the north by Cumberland Ave) 25% were built before 1885. KHA "Real Property Inventory," pt. 3, p. 52.

women sold eggs, shelled walnuts, jams and honey. Permanent butcher and flower and fruit stalls and restaurants and lunch counters on each side. They walked along the sidewalks flanking the modest house where produce and flower trucks, mostly canvas-covered Ford pickups of the thirties, were parked, backed up to the curbs, their overladen tailgates hanging heavy, the country folks standing by ready to sack up some pole beans and okra.[24]

An even more heightened sense of Knoxville's physical landscape, both along the riverfront and in its older core, was supplied in the evocative descriptions of Cormac McCarthy's *Suttree* (1979), set in Knoxville of the 1950s. No native of Knoxville has drawn as vibrant a picture of the city as McCarthy, who portrayed it as a sleazy, gritty collection of disheveled dwellings, shanties, and played-out people whose collective failure was etched into their faces and minds. Poverty, alcoholism, and hopelessness marked McCarthy's Knoxville every bit as much as did the coal dust.[25]

Madden and McCarthy both confirmed the observations of Gunther and Templeton, as did the 1939 housing survey and remembrances of other Knoxvillians, such as those of the late Knoxville businessman-artist Russell Briscoe. But, like Gunther, all seem to have missed the causes of these physical problems as well as the historical and demographic forces that made it difficult for Knoxvillians to respond to them. Simply put, Knoxville failed to build on its wartime rejuvenation after the war, as local industries did not participate in the general postwar economic upswing. Simultaneously, lack of economic opportunities prompted general out-migration from the city, while people coming into the area were settling beyond the city limits in the burgeoning suburban fringe. Investment capital, therefore, tended to be attracted to the fringe and out of the core which, without regular injections of money and care, began to deteriorate physically. Nor could the city government offer assistance, with a high proportion of its revenue committed to retiring earlier bond issues (the payments on some of which had been suspended during the Depression) and with insufficient surplus capital to take on beautification or improvement projects. As the nation boomed, then, Knoxville remained a troubled city.

And demographically, statistics concerning those who remained in Knoxville during the 1940s augured ill for the city beyond the postwar

---

[24] Madden, *Bijou*, 92.

[25] In Madden's *Bijou* and his short-story collection *The Shadow Knows*, as well as in *Suttree*, the contradictions and conflicts between the urban milieu of Knoxville and the values and cultures of rural Appalachia are constantly evoked. Nowhere is this more vibrantly depicted than in "God Proud," Madden's short story, or in the segments of McCarthy's novel where Suttree purges himself by wandering through the Smoky Mountains. See "God Proud," *The Shadow Knows* (Baton Rouge, 1963), 124–56; Cormac McCarthy, *Suttree* (New York, 1979).

decade. In the 1940s blacks, poor whites, and the elderly constituted an increasing share of Knoxville's population. In that decade white population increased 10.6 percent while the city's black population rose by 19.3 percent. In wards with high proportions of blacks, unemployment and poverty were considerably more widespread, for blacks were traditionally closed out of jobs in the skilled construction and retail trade fields, which in the North and the South almost exclusively hired whites. Median annual income of non-white city dwellers, at $1,443 (1947), was nearly $1,000 less than that enjoyed by the city as a whole. In 1948 for the first time since the 1930s homicide became a leading cause of death.[26]

In stark contrast to the inner city, Ward Twenty-four, which contains Sequoyah Hills, was characteristic of the areas to which the prosperous industrial bourgeoisie was fleeing. Annexed in 1917 and occupying the bend in the Tennessee River west of Third Creek and above Looney's Island, this community planned for Knoxville's "better" elements had, in 1939, 858 residential structures, of which nearly 700 had been built since 1915 and about half since 1925. Two-thirds of the units in the ward had at least one bath and toilet, over half were described in 1934 as being in good condition, and over half paid rents or their equivalents of more than $50 per month.[27]

In earlier decades, rich and poor, white and black had lived fairly close to one another. Even today, one can see the architectural evidence of this in the neighborhoods of Fourth and Gill (a few blocks north of downtown and east of Broadway); Happy Hollow (north of downtown and west of Broadway); the East Scott–Oklahoma Avenue area (north of downtown and east of Central); and Mechanicsville, where Welsh iron workers built imposing Victorian residences side-by-side with modest shotgun houses usually occupied by blacks. But after World War II the city increasingly became fragmented into enclaves of class and race. To be sure, this trend had begun as early as the 1880s, when more well-to-do Knoxvillians fled the city for the more exclusive neighborhood of West Knoxville (now Fort Sanders), or in the 1920s, when Sequoyah Hills and Talahi were developed. However, the dramatic acceleration of this trend after World War II confronted the city with even greater dilemmas than it had faced before.

Other cities tried to overcome similar problems by annexing the suburban

[26]*Journal*, Apr. 14, 1948. "Knoxville is one of the very few, if not the only large city in the U.S. where homicide is among the first 10 chief causes of death." Twenty years previously it had not even been listed.

[27]KHA, "Real Property Inventory," block tabulations for Ward 24, p. 75. Wards gaining and losing in population between 1940 and 1950 adequately spell out the emergence of two cities—with dramatic losses in the poorer inner-city wards (1, 2, 3, 4, 6, 9, and 11), some losing as much as 50% of their population, contrasted with high-growth wards to the west (10 and 24, the latter the fastest growing in the city) and to the northeast (12 and 16). Actual gains and losses are tabulated in *News-Sentinel*, Oct. 1, 1950.

fringes almost as fast as people settled in them. Knoxville, however, had not annexed territory since 1917, and by the late 1940s the real city had spread far beyond its artificial but crucial civil boundaries. Knoxville's political leaders religiously avoided any annexation in which the city would be required to provide services (education, fire and police protection, garbage collection, and sewers) that they felt would offset potential increases in revenues. Instead, politicians cried for lower taxes, even at the risk of being unable to raise money for physical improvements. Simultaneously, they engaged in brutal personal political warfare, the results of which left the city virtually unchanged by the end of the decade.

THE POLITICS OF PAROCHIALISM

If political form and style is the mirror of a city's character, then Knoxville of the 1940s was a dark glass indeed. A popular characterization of the city—"Knoxville, where the girls are the grandest and politics the damnedest"—suggested the almost impenetrable nature of the city's politics, marked by ever-shifting alliances and an almost total disregard for issues of substance. In this milieu of the 1940s the two dominant political figures were Caswell Orton (Cas) Walker and George Dempster. Although political enemies most of the time (Dempster is alleged to have said, "If I ordered a whole carload of sob's and they just sent Cas, I'd sign for the shipment")[28] and from radically different social and economic backgrounds, both Dempster and Walker embraced a political style that alternately amused and outraged Knoxville's citizenry. Both avoided facing the real issues that seemed to weaken the troubled city.

George Dempster (1887–1964) was a native Knoxvillian whose father had been a partner in a city grist mill. During his early teens George worked as a laborer on the railroads and as a steam-shovel operator on the Panama Canal. Upon his return to Knoxville, Dempster and several of his brothers founded the Dempster Construction Company, which specialized in heavy road and grading work and later pioneered in producing an ingenious and efficient garbage pickup system known as the Dempster Dumpster. A successful and prominent industrialist, Dempster is remembered as a local philanthropist and a tireless crusader for urban physical improvements. In private a tasteful and cultured individual (his opponent Walker liked to characterize him as a member of "the silk-stocking crowd"), Dempster nevertheless possessed an often outrageous and dramatic political style that had its local appeal. Faced with a councilmanic revolt in which Dempster

---

[28] Todd Baker, "The Politics of Innovation" (Ph. D. diss., Univ. of Tennessee, Knoxville, 1968), 115.

George Dempster (right)

PHOTOGRAPH TAKEN FOR *Fortune* BY
LOUIS SCHLIVEK

asserted that there were members of the city council who would like to kill him, Dempster strode to the dais in a public council meeting, turned his back on the council, raised his coattails, and dared them to "shoot him where the galluses crossed." Such political rough-and-tumble paid off enough for Dempster to have become city manager twice and mayor once.[29]

Cas Walker (1903–), though outwardly less sophisticated than Dempster, was a master of East Tennessee political style and was what one writer has called the "latest of a line of hillbilly politicians," one of the practitioners of an East Tennessee mountain politics described as "highly personal, bitter, at times disrespectful of the truth of the matter and flamboyant." Born in neighboring Sevier County, Cas Walker came to Knoxville in the spring of 1924, via the coalfields of Kentucky. This self-styled "po' boy," who would come to glory in the media's image of him as a redneck, a "barefooted bootlegger," and a humble coal miner, publicly posed, as he puts it, "as a kinder idiot" and political underdog battling the reformist elites of the city's politics whom he called the "silk-stocking crowd."

The shrewdness, native sagacity, and horse-trading mentality that were part of Walker's political image in later years he had come by honestly as a businessman. Setting up in a small shop with a relative, Walker learned to specialize in the business "come-on." Advertising Coca-Cola at bargain rates but purchasing cheap bottled soda from Kentucky, Walker hid the Coke at the bottom of the cooler under ice, loaded the cooler with the cheaper drinks, purchased heavily salted peanuts and popcorn, "locked the back door so nobody could get at the water," and proceeded to turn a profit on the thirsty customers who came for Coca-Cola but purchased Strawberry Surprise. Walker went on to establish a chain of grocery stores that he promoted by throwing chickens off the roof to assembled multitudes on Saturdays and hiring a black "who could dance up a storm" for entertainment and a bail bondsman to keep him from being put in jail for traffic obstruction.[30] An avid coon dog fancier, Walker was struck by the cheapness of tick and flea dip for dogs, and one of his promotional schemes at a Pennington Gap, Virginia, store was to give away dog dip with every ten-dollar grocery order. The first three dollars covered Cas's initial investment for nearly unlimited hound dips, whereas the ten-dollar grocery orders were incremental.

One of the high points in regional advertising came when Walker's lawyer suggested a cheap contract between Walker and "Digger O'Dell," an out-of-work entrepreneur who promised to be buried alive in Walker's grocery store parking lot as an advertising gimmick. Burying a refrigerator to keep Digger cool (although the machine was unconnected) and feeding him soup through a straw, Walker obtained endorsements from Campbell's Soup and

[29]*Journal*, Nov. 3, 1939.
[30]Cas Walker, Lecture, Knoxville History class, July 3, 1980.

Frigidaire. A nearby drug store paid Walker for the franchise to sell "Diggerburgers." The products did better than the person in question, who, allegedly having signed the contract under the influence of alcohol, hastily repented of his premature burial and entered a plea of sickness. Walker, for whom a contract remained sacred but who feared that an actual burial might follow a media one, hired nurses to sit in vigil over the recumbent Digger and drove a stovepipe to the casket for more air. The masses, who Walker alleges came to see someone die but were too embarrassed to admit it, bought groceries in record amounts. As Walker says, "The register never stopped ringing." So many queries came from the curious crowds about the purpose of the stovepipe that Walker had it painted red, attached a separate container to it, and advertised it as a "wishing well" for the recumbent Digger's continued good health. The wishing well attracted media coverage and along with the endorsements, the Diggerburger franchises, and the grocery sales, netted a tidy profit.[31] Walker's financial and promotional style was father to his political style.

Walker, who gloried in the rough-and-tumble of one-on-one political confrontation, was in many respects not a traditional party man. He says that politics appealed to him because he liked the "challenge." In many respects the "challenge" of politics was little different from that of the competitive business world he engaged in as grocer and entrepreneur. In fact, the two worlds were in a sense symbiotic—political exposure was good for business and vice versa. And the same sharp practices could be useful in either. Walker, after his retirement from politics, said that he and others on the city council had used secret signals to hold up issues in council so they could be resolved later among cronies by "common sense." He argued, "If you don't get a little shady in politics, you never get in the sunshine." No stranger to the use of media in business, ironically Walker later came to abhor the slickness of media politics, arguing after his active years in politics that things were now different and that he could "run one of his coon dogs and get it elected."[32]

Walker's entrance into Knoxville politics coincided with Louis Brownlow's defeat as city manager. In some respects this was advantageous to Walker, for in the years ahead, as Knoxville moved away from Brownlow's managerial tactics and his taste for efficiency and planning, the city reverted to a more traditional political course, and one well suited to Walker's tastes. In other respects, however, Brownlow and his supporters had firmly lodged in Knoxville's political conscience a penchant for planning which—city manager or no—was to result in the formation of the KHA, the KTL, the KUB, and many similar institutions. Planning, however beneficial in the long run,

[31] Ibid.
[32] Ibid.

was costly, and in light of the city's chronic indebtedness, increased fiscal outlays were as much anathema to Walker as they had been to that earlier enemy of managerial reform, Lee Monday, who had hounded Louis Brownlow into resignation. In fact, Walker stated in one interview that he began in politics by supporting Monday against Brownlow, although later on two occasions he publicly denied knowing Monday. Ideologically, the two were cut from the same cloth. In 1939 George Dempster asked Walker to join a "progressive" (i.e., anti-administration) city council ticket. It is said that politics makes strange bedfellows but surely none stranger than these. Most likely, Dempster realized that Walker's popularity in the black neighborhoods where most of his stores operated and the popularity created by his flamboyant advertising style had made him well known, a potential vote-getter. Walker, with his own brand of humorous self-deprecation, says simply that Dempster liked him as a candidate because he (Walker) referred to an incumbent councilman as being "as confused as the boy who dropped his chewing gum on the hen house floor," thus appealing to Dempster's businessman-cum-redneck side.[33] Claiming he did not want to run with Dempster (whom he now describes as "strictly honest . . . but mean, real mean"), Walker demonstrated his ideological debt to Monday by running as a virtual independent under the slogan "For lower taxes, vote for and elect Cas Walker." In his first bid for office, Walker did not place high enough for a seat—a loss he would not repeat.[34]

By 1941 Walker's political style was well established. Sagaciously using newspaper and radio advertisements combining his grocery business with his political views, Walker was able to gain wide name recognition and to create the impression that he (like so many of his constituents) was the underdog battling against the rich and well born—as well as against the large supermarket chains.

"People like the underdog," Walker later admitted. "I played like the poor boy, like I was just gettin' along . . . people played me a long time for a kinder idiotic person." Those familiar with the politics of Knoxville were not among them. Walker's constituency was significant, and he was an important man to anyone seeking office in Knoxville.[35]

Walker was especially successful in the black wards of the city. Always denying that he bought up hundreds of poll tax receipts ("people gave 'em to me for safekeepin' . . . I would hold their slips and vote 'em the way I could"), he also claimed he gave the city's blacks the proper ballots to be

[33]Ibid. For Walker's support of Monday against Brownlow, see Walker interview, Feb. 21, 1977.

[34]*Journal*, Oct. 22, 1939.

[35]Walker interview, Feb. 21, 1977. On Walker's significance in municipal politics, see interview with Lee Greene, Professor Emeritus, Department of Political Science, University of Tennessee, Feb. 15, 1977.

kept in their hats and to be used once inside the polls ("blacks like to think they're gettin' away with something"). The grocer politician was able to muster support from frustrated blacks, for whom the city was no place of opportunity, by applying to campaigns his successful advertising strategies. He had "chittlin and pigs' feet parties" in the black wards ("The best way in the world to get people to vote for yuh is to feed 'em"). Asked about the 1940s version of media blitz, Walker said he would go out to the black areas "with pigs' feet, tails, neckbones, [and] have a real shindig." At these parties he would appear in person and give a little speech ("Pig ears and snouts sure get a lot of votes"). Hardly textbook cases of good campaigning, Walker's tactics were nonetheless effective. Some charged that Walker used to visit black churches and ostentatiously contribute to their building or mortgage funds.[36]

Walker's style paid off, for in the 1941 city council balloting he led the list of vote-getters. More significantly, he led in virtually every black area of the city, as he would in almost every election throughout the next two decades. But Walker's tactics were not directed just at the black vote. In the poorer sections, where street conditions were abysmal, Walker would find out a day in advance from an informant at the city garage where the street repair crews were scheduled to work. At the appointed place and time, candidate Walker was there ahead of the road crew, highly visible and leaving the impression that he personally was seeing to his constituents' well-being. On one occasion, campaigning against the bootleg joints and "rough places" that flourished in the dry city, Walker arranged to have coteries of drunks loiter about his opponent's headquarters on polling day; in his own vicinity, of course, were numerous Appalachian versions of Shirley Temple, dressed in white pinafores and wearing blue ribbons emblazoned "Vote for my Uncle Cas"—proof enough that he was on the side of sobriety.[37]

Although technically an independent in politics, Walker was in fact allied with Dempster in the 1939, 1941, and 1943 city council races. Walker recalls that "Dempster always knew he needed me to win" and that "me 'n' Dempster got along good." However, when Dempster (with Walker's aid) became city manager again in 1944, a rift developed. As city manager, Dempster found it necessary to seek additional revenue sources and proposed a limited personal property tax. As Walker put it, "Dempster was a good councilman, but when he went for city manager and went for personal property tax, I couldn't afford to be for that." Walker obviously could not, since he had

[36]Walker interview, Feb. 21, 1977; lecture to Knoxville History class, July 3, 1980.

[37]*News-Sentinel*, Nov. 7, 1941. In 1943, when he was once again a top vote-getter, Walker attacked the *Journal* for its attempts to alienate the black voters from him. For the "Uncle Cas" story, Cas Walker interview, Feb. 21, 1977, and lecture in Knoxville History class, July 3, 1980.

spent virtually all his time flaying the rich businessmen who, he charged, had avoided paying their full taxes while the poor had paid full assessments. He claimed that the city would have plenty of operating capital if only the rich were assessed real property taxes as evenly as the poor. Walker remembered that in a stormy private meeting the city manager (referring to their mutual campaign promise of no more taxes) exclaimed, "To hell with the platform—it's only made to *run* on!" Walker's resulting open opposition to Dempster in a city council session finally blew apart their shaky alliance. Yet, because the grocer-politician was the stronger of the two in terms of political style and voter base, he lost little by his rift with the popular and progressive city manager.[38]

Indeed, by 1943 Walker was so powerful that he was virtually uncontrollable, despite the fact that the middle- and upper-class voters were beginning to find his style an embarrassment. One wrote angrily to the Knoxville *Journal* in 1943 when Walker was being considered for mayor: "Do we want a mayor who by his own admission has amassed a fortune, yet . . . tries to make the lower-income citizens believe they are being swindled and exploited by those with a little more money? Or that every man with an extra pair of socks is a predatory capitalist, who spends most of his time devising means to suck the life-blood out of the working people[?]"[39] The civic-commercial elite grumbled that Walker was becoming less amusing and that "something would have to be done about him." For his part, Walker laughed off his growing unpopularity in the middle- and upper-class wards ("they hated to think that they was voting for some coal miner").[40]

Walker should not have taken the rumors so lightly. True, his support was unshaken in the black wards and improving in the poor white ones. Yet such successes had come in city elections in which there had been virtually no significant opposition from the civic-commercial elite and in which voter turnouts had been low. In 1946 both of these conditions would change.

Finally (after he successfully defeated at-large candidates) the council was forced to give Walker the mayoralty, a post he grandly assumed in 1946 (the *News-Sentinel* commented drily that he had taken to wearing a necktie since he was first discussed for mayor).[41] Walker's elevation to mayor virtually sealed Dempster's fate as city manager, a post he resigned in order to deny Walker the pleasure of discharging him.

[38]On Walker's attack on the property-tax assessments of the rich, see *News-Sentinel*, Oct. 20, 23, 27, 1943; *Journal*, Nov. 4, 1943. For Walker's recollections of the Dempster-Walker break see Walker interview, Feb. 21, 1977.

[39]*Journal*, Nov. 3, 1943. The city charter provided that the mayor was to be chosen from the city council by the council members. With the city-manager form of government, the office of mayor was largely intended to be a ceremonial one. See *News-Sentinel*, Nov. 2, 1946.

[40]Walker interview, Feb. 21, 1977.

[41]*News-Sentinel*, Nov. 16, 1945.

But despite the rout of his political foes, Walker's problems had just begun. Now he was mayor and no longer able to talk with impunity and conviction about being an outsider. Now he was obliged to do more than criticize. He was obliged to take care of his supporters, many of whom hungered for city offices. Now he had to try to solve such thorny problems as taxes, the city's massive bonded indebtedness, zoning, and unemployment.[42]

Thus, to remain consistent as well as faithful to his constituents, the grocer-politician was, within a month, forced to oppose the city manager whom he himself had appointed. The new city manager, Paul Morton, refused to give way to Walker on political appointments, spot rezoning, or the city budget, which included funds for Morton's ambitious plans to get Knoxville moving again. By February 1946 the break was open, with Morton politicking for his program before civic clubs and Walker harassing the city manager before council and his constituents. As expected, Walker won, slashing Morton's budget and smilingly cutting taxes.[43]

In March the civic-commercial elite was finally sufficiently aroused to form what it called the Good Government Group, an ill-disguised organization to back Morton. Boasting a distinguished roster of officers and directors, the group took as its charge the "encouragement of qualified candidates for office," a thinly veiled warning to the boisterous mayor.[44]

Finally, after less than eleven weeks in his post, Morton was doomed. On March 19, in a wild city council session, Walker and his council friends voted to dismiss the stubborn city manager. Within hours cries for Walker's recall were heard, principally from people who apparently had been waiting for this misstep by the grocer-mayor. A Citizens Protective League, formed largely from Good Government Group members, nominated lumber company executive Edward Chavannes to oppose Walker in the December recall election and called for the removal of two Walker allies on the council as well. Ironically, the *News-Sentinel*, in comparing the ouster of Morton to the forcing out of Louis Brownlow twenty years before, failed to remember that a protégé of Lee Monday had helped bring about that 1926 resignation.[45]

The 1946 campaign was probably the dirtiest in Knoxville's modern

[42]Ibid., Jan. 13, 14, 1946.

[43]Ibid., Jan. 7, 1946. It was said by Walker's opponents that he favored spot rezoning so that he could build a new store on East Magnolia Avenue. Ibid., Feb. 5, 1946.

[44]Ibid., Mar. 3, 1946. Walker had more troubles than these. In 1944 the Knoxville *Journal* had accused the grocer of being a "flagrant OPA violator," a charge that Walker answered with a libel suit. In the midst of the Morton-Walker fray the case was decided against Walker. Ibid., Jan. 29, 1946.

[45]*News-Sentinel*, Mar. 20, 1946; on Chavannes, see ibid., Nov. 25, 1946. On the comparison of Morton's ouster to Brownlow's, see ibid., Nov. 19, 1946.

memory of savage political contests. Walker was opposed by virtually every elite social and business organization, from the Junior Chamber of Commerce to the Knoxville Garden Club. He was lambasted as a "champion for nobody but himself" (a slur on his image as the workingman's friend), a "political accident" of low voter turnout in city elections, a political meddler, and a mayor who in nine months had accomplished nothing except virtually bankrupting the city and reaping "a harvest of nation-wide ridicule for this community." Local newspapers quoted anti-Walker forces:

> The mayor's duties are chiefly ceremonial. He is the city's spokesman and official greeter. . . . Mayor Cas Walker does not meet any of the requirements of the office which he sought for so many years. In fact, he has seldom performed as the city's official greeter for obvious reasons. Instead, he used the office to advertise his private business, to promote his personal political fortunes, and even to advance the cause of a macaroni maker.[46]

In such a bare-knuckled battle, Walker's political style was at its best. Claiming that the afternoon paper, a Scripps-Howard publication which Walker erroneously called "the New York Chain Newspaper," opposed him because Morton had lowered its tax assessment by $25,000, Walker held meetings throughout the city, serving familiar refreshments, providing country music, and attacking "the silk-stocking crowd." He even claimed that the principal charges against him were that he did not have a college degree and that he was not a polished, educated-sounding speaker, points designed to strike home with his constituency.[47]

But Walker could not stand against an aroused and united civic-commercial elite. While his own wards did not desert him, abnormally high voter turnout in other areas of the city and the last-minute opposition of George Dempster defeated him and his two councilman allies. Walker carried thirteen of the city's forty-one wards, principally those areas inhabited by the black and white working-class population that had always stood by him. But Chavannes piled up such enormous majorities in what Walker referred to as the "silk-stocking" neighborhoods that he won going away.[48]

Although such a defeat would normally spell the end for a politician, for Walker it was but a temporary setback. As the civic-commercial elite naively withdrew once again to its offices and homes, it left the city to the grocer-politician, who was willing to work full time and who used his own political style to such advantage. Within ten months Walker was back on the city council, finishing first among eight candidates and never dropping below

[46]*News-Sentinel*, Nov. 2, 16, 18, 20, 24, Dec. 1, 1946.
[47]Ibid., Nov. 20, 23, Dec. 1, 1946.
[48]Ibid., Dec. 4, 1946.

fourth place in any ward. Throughout the 1940s and 1950s Cas Walker continued to win office and to oppose virtually every idea or move advocated by the elite, usually on the grounds that it would raise the workingman's taxes.

In 1950, barely three years after his own recall, Walker was powerful enough to scuttle plans for a new city-county building. The building was a dream of Mayor James Elmore, Jr., who, like many politicians before and after him, discovered that Walker's style and name made him virtually invincible in the city. Indeed, as the economic woes of the 1950s crept across the troubled city, Walker's power increased almost in direct proportion to the increase in levels of unemployment and economic suffering in black and poor white neighborhoods. So it had always been with Walker.

In retrospect, Knoxville politics during the tumultuous 1940s seems to display an air of unreality. Strong signs that manufacturing was not growing fast enough to keep up with job demand, suburbanization, and general physical deterioration were crucial issues crying out to be addressed. Yet Knoxville's political barons ignored these momentous problems, preferring to hack ferociously at each other with ill-disguised glee. Faced with the challenge of leading the city out of its malaise, instead they bowed to the fearful and dispirited voters' wishes for low taxes and limited change. The city manager system, which might have planned and executed an urban rejuvenation program, was mortally wounded in the bloody political battles of the postwar years. Political life would change in Knoxville in the years ahead, but in the 1940s it appeared narrow, parochial, and visionless.

THE NEW AND THE OLD—OAK RIDGE AND KNOXVILLE

As Knoxville seemed unable to participate in the general national economic upsurge of the 1940s, it must have galled some Knoxvillians to know that but a few miles away a new city—also to be in the new Knoxville Standard Metropolitan Statistical Area (SMSA) in 1950—supported by a new industry was burgeoning. Founded in 1942, Oak Ridge was initially a "city behind a fence," the site of the Manhattan Project dedicated to building the first atomic bomb. Demands for nearly all types of workers caused the new city's wartime population to reach a peak of 75,000. Though in the postwar years that population would dwindle (Oak Ridge's 1980 population was approximately 27,000), in the immediate postwar period there was no hint of the future decline. All that Knoxvillians knew was that Oak Ridgers seemed to have an almost inexhaustible supply of money and an almost insatiable demand for food, clothing, strong drink, and luxuries.[49]

[49]On wartime Oak Ridge see Johnson and Jackson, *City Behind a Fence.*

Consciously and unconsciously, Knoxvillians sensed that Oak Ridge represented a future that would be denied their own city. To those few Knoxvillians who saw that Knoxville was dropping behind its southern competitors and who searched frantically for a way to reverse that trend, the coattails of Oak Ridge seemed not only a convenience but also a godsend. A *News-Sentinel* editorial of August 7, 1945, mixing unpardonable xeno-phobia with furious back-slapping, first publicly proffered this coattails ploy: "Detroit has only been known as the auto capital of the world; New York is the financial capital; Pittsburg the steel center. Knoxville may well become known as the capital city of atomic energy." The editorial went on to remind Knoxvillians that they stood on the threshold of a new era: "citizens of this community must realize by now that a busy and exciting future confronts us—the "old timers," the newcomers, and the thousands of tem-porary residents who may be planning to stay on here. . . ."[50]

But Oak Ridgers bridled at being associated with what many of them felt was a dying provincial city. One Oak Ridger replied to the editorial: "By what earthly right do you have the gall to suggest that Knoxville may well become known as the capital city of atomic energy?" and chided the editor for "the most flagrant case of jumping on the band wagon that I have ever witnessed." Such ill will was typical of the war years. Knoxvillians, it was alleged, had "jacked up" prices for "foreigners" and "outsiders": "We have been here since March, 1944, and not once can I say I ever got a square deal in Knoxville."

Miss W—— D—— was in a like frame of mind: "We were treated with scorn and looked upon as so many aliens to be bled dry by local merchants . . . we were charged exorbitant prices for food, rent, clothing and even at that you Knoxvillians had griped that the OPA had put a price ceiling on these things and you were not allowed to charge more. . . . Don't you think that after three years it's a little bit late to welcome us to Knoxville? Aren't you afraid that Knoxville might eventually be absorbed by Oak Ridge?" She then struck what was, for many Knoxvillians, a tenderer spot:

> Practically all of the workers of Oak Ridge came here from cosmopoli-tan cities, cities that extend a hearty welcome to newcomers, cities that had something to offer in the way of entertainment and recreation. But in Knoxville we saw old shows, we ran into your blue laws, we found ourselves on Sundays as strangers in an inhospitable town with nothing to do. We found your sidewalks rolled up at night the few nights we were able to leave the reservation in search of diversion.[51]

Stung by the Gunther-like attacks, startled and outraged Knoxvillians

[50]*News-Sentinel*, Aug. 7, 1945: "Knoxville—Capital City of Atomic Energy."
[51]Ibid., Aug. 10, 1945.

replied as best they could, heaping abuse on Oak Ridgers while defending their stagnant city. Knoxvillians were quick to respond that they, too, had suffered through the same wartime problems as others, and that housing shortages, scarcities, rationing, and standing in lines were tortures not exclusively reserved for Oak Ridgers visiting Knoxville. Admitting that Knoxville was not cosmopolitan like the cities Oak Ridgers hailed from and that·it was a "one-horse town," Mrs. P—— W—— of Fountain City insisted that home, in the last analysis, was what you made of it. Mrs. B. C—— of Knoxville was less apologetic: "As for entertainment and recreation on Sunday here in Knoxville, we have plenty of churches to attend. There are more religious and God-fearing people in Knoxville than most cities, and I hope we continue to have it that way." If foolish boosterism could open Knoxvillians to the barbs of Oak Ridgers over the "energy capital" syndrome, other Knoxvillians could draw upon traditional values to defend their city in the argument that ensued.[52]

The editorial-page war may have shed more heat than light. But beneath the stinging insults of those who reviled Knoxville as backward and unmodern, there was another reality, heralded by the atomic age that had recently made its debut at Hiroshima. The city was frozen in an earlier industrial era. D—— B—— of Oak Ridge was aghast that Knoxville could tout itself as the "capital city of Atomic Energy." The closest thing to atomic energy in Knoxville, he asserted, was a perfume atomizer. "You [Knoxvillians] have been floating in a castle on a cloud for a long time. The blast that Clinton Engineer Works dealt Japan ought to awaken Knoxvillians from their sweet slumber of reveries." D—— B—— suggested that Knoxvillians richly deserved for their city's title "The Gateway to Oak Ridge." The penultimate letter published in the ongoing debate must have rankled Knoxvillians more than any other, for its writer commented, "I am a native of Nashville and I always thought it was the most dirty, inhospitable, and corrupt city that ever was until I moved here. But Knoxville has Nashville beat a mile."[53]

The *News-Sentinel* editor remarked that the discussions of "long-suppressed feelings" by Oak Ridgers and Knoxvillians "have been revealing and interesting but prolonged discussion would not be desirable" and he cut off the debate.[54] Prolonged discussion might well have revealed that the "long-suppressed" feelings were perhaps not long-suppressed at all, but were rather a fairly new recognition of the fact that in the wartime decade Knoxville at heart remained an older Appalachian industrial city.

In the end, Knoxville could not shake off the memory of John Gunther. He haunted the city. As Americans generally, if not universally, basked in

[52]Ibid., Aug. 14, 1945.
[53]Ibid., Aug. 15, 1945.
[54]Ibid., Aug. 16, 1945.

postwar prosperity and feared communism at home as well as abroad, Knoxville remained a city imprisoned in time, unable either to identify or cut loose from its fetters. Worse, suburbanization, core deterioration, lackluster economic growth, and political parochialism presaged even more troubled times ahead. As Knoxvillians in turn attacked or ignored their critics, from Gunther to the irate Oak Ridgers, they appeared to lack the energy to do anything other.

CHAPTER THREE ★ *Coming Unraveled: Suburbanization,
Industrial Decline, and
Political Malaise*

IN 1957 the talk of the University of Tennessee's theater season was an original play by young drama professor Paul Soper. His production, *Once Upon a Town*, was an ill-disguised satire on the political life of "one of them prohibition towns in Tennessee," obviously Knoxville. The idealistic city manager, played broadly by Bob Mashburn, continually struggled against an ultra-conservative, parochial, and visionless city council, one of whose members proudly asserted, "Some of us is self-made." UT's Carousel Theater was packed for every performance, and the play's brief run had to be extended to accommodate all those who wanted to join in mocking the city's own government. Ultimately Soper's hit outdrew *Arsenic and Old Lace*, *Sabrina Fair*, and *My Three Angels*.[1]

Whether Knoxvillians chose to laugh at their own government, worry over the forces that seemed to paralyze the city, hope that the modest physical improvements that did come were harbingers of better things ahead, or simply ignore the whole question, Knoxville during the 1950s was obviously a city in trouble. Never having participated fully in the nation's postwar economic recovery, Knoxville was now battered by developments over which it seemed to have little control: decline in manufacturing, rapid deterioration of its downtown core, suburbanization, and the impact of the automobile culture. While some attempted to reverse those trends, their attempts were frustrated by a badly fragmented political structure that lacked the will or power to effect profound changes. Hence, although some Knox-villians crowded into the Carousel Theater to delight in Soper's lampoon, the city's plight clearly was no laughing matter.

AMERICAN CITIES IN THE 1950s

The Eisenhower administration inherited a national economy going at full tilt, thanks largely to postwar rejuvenation, Cold War spending, and Tru-

[1] *News-Sentinel*, Mar. 24, 1957. The article stated: "Dr. Soper says carefully that no parody on Knoxville is intended. But leave us not play ostrich." An Apr. 3, 1957, article, after having noted the success of the play, described it as one in which "local political shenanigans get a working over." Ibid., Apr. 3, 1957.

man's continuation and extension of many New Deal programs. In an effort to "split the difference between Coolidge and Keynes," Eisenhower hoped to keep the economy healthy while controlling the rate of inflation and turning some fiscal and economic responsibilities back to the private sector. While Eisenhower did keep the annual inflation rate at a low 2.5 percent, the costs of his doing so included increased unemployment (peaking in the spring of 1958 at 7.6 percent) and three brief but sharp recessions, in 1953–1954, 1957–1958, and 1960–1961.[2]

On the surface, however, it seemed the most prosperous and comfortable of decades. If the Cold War or the civil rights struggle occasionally intruded to disturb the general complacence, most Americans were comforted by their new material possessions and higher standard of living. Indeed, by 1960 the nation's per capita income was 35 percent above that of 1945, and affluence appeared so widespread that some believed the United States was rapidly moving toward the eradication of want and the creation of a classless society. Michael Harrington's *The Other America*, a study that symbolically marks the "rediscovery" of poverty, did not appear until 1962. For most Americans, especially those of the new middle class who had used the GI bill and economic expansion to gain upward mobility, the 1950s were wonderful if insecure times.[3]

Three interrelated trends highlighted the 1950s: suburbanization, the rise in installment buying, and the increasingly pervasive influence of television. Suburbs boomed as the new middle class sought to escape from the cities to the newer, cleaner, more homogeneous, and safer urban fringes. Aided by the automobile (which made suburbs possible) and by installment buying (which made those suburbs appear more affluent than they were), the new suburban communities acted as magnets, pulling a willing people toward a new style of life. For its part, television lionized suburban living with programs featuring model homes, model parents, model children, and model possessions. From *Father Knows Best* to *Leave It to Beaver*, television extolled the virtues of suburbia, where automobiles were large and problems were small. As suburbanites turned to television for enjoyment, recreation,and babysitting services, they recognized themselves and saw that all was well. If John Cameron Swayze, Douglas Edwards, or Howard K. Smith briefly disturbed their reveries, they had only to wait a few moments to be comforted once again.

Clearly, then, suburbanization was more than simply a mass migration into newer homes on the urban fringe. In fact, it was nothing less than a new

[2]Alonzo L. Hamby, *The Imperial Years: The United States Since 1939* (New York, 1976), 181–82.

[3]William E. Leuchtenberg, ed., *The Unfinished Century: America Since 1900* (Boston, 1973), 680, 724.

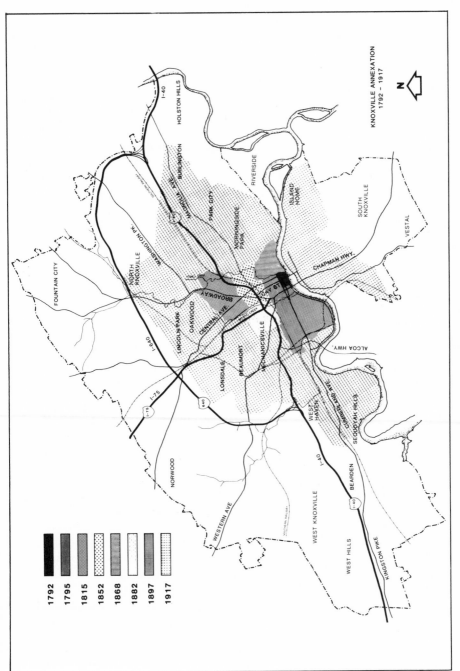

III. Knoxville Annexations, 1792–1917

attitude and way of life. The fearfulness of the Great Depression had disappeared entirely, and between 1946 and 1958 short-term consumer credit climbed from $8.4 billion to almost $45 billion. To profit from this new, credit-based affluence, retail merchants followed the mass migration into increasingly ostentatious shopping centers rapidly being thrown up in the suburbs. Some churches, too, followed their parishioners, as did YMCAs, YWCAs, Boy Scouts, and Girl Scouts. Suburbanites found fewer and fewer reasons to return to the core cities from which many of them had come. Sapped of population, energy, and tax revenue, American cities in the 1950s became troubled pockets of people, exceptions to what John Kenneth Galbraith in 1958 called *The Affluent Society*.[4]

ECONOMIC DISLOCATION AND DEMOGRAPHIC MALAISE

Troubles, of course, were nothing new to Knoxville. From 1900 on, the city had defined its central work function as manufacturing, and, as with Birmingham and Richmond, manufacturing had assumed increasing importance for Knoxville throughout the twentieth century. But the Great Depression and the city's failure to participate in the general postwar boom had left Knoxville in a precarious economic position, ill prepared to face the changes to come in the 1950s.

Table 1, from the Hammer report shows the structure of manufacturing employment in the Knoxville metropolitan area. The first group, "old-line" southern industries, were heavily concentrated in the city of Knoxville proper, especially the textile mills, which ranked just behind the "new line" southern industries of ALCOA and the Atomic Energy Commission (AEC), both outside the city in the metro area.

Preeminent among those changes was the decline, for the apparel industry, of the types of manufacturing upon which the city's economy rested. Textiles were especially troubled, as between 1948 and 1960 nearly 3,000 jobs were lost in that industry alone. In 1954, in the midst of what the city's mayor called a "general slump" in one of the city's most important industrial sectors, the Cherokee Textile Mills and Venus Hosiery Mills announced that they were leaving Knoxville. At the same time, the city tax commission, fearful that Brookside Mills, one of the big textile employers, might leave the city, slashed the mill's personalty assessment by over $250,000 and reduced its realty assessment by over $100,000. Yet Brookside Mills was doomed, a victim of outdated machinery, the high costs of modernization, and increased competition. Trying desperately to save itself, in 1954 Brookside announced a 5-percent wage cut, then whittled the number of employees

[4]Ibid., 717.

TABLE 1. *Changes in Manufacturing Employment in the Metropolitan Knoxville Economy, 1948–60*

	NUMBER OF EMPLOYEES (000)		1948–60 CHANGE	
	1948	1960	NUMBER	PERCENT
"Old-Line" Southern Industries				
Apparel	2.9	4.1	1,200	41.4%
Textiles	8.3	5.4	−2,900	−34.9
Lumber	1.4	0.6	− 800	−57.1
Furniture	0.6	0.5	− 100	−16.7
Subtotal	(13.2)	(10.6)	(−2,600)	−19.7
"New-Line" Southern Industries				
Chemicals: AEC operations only	10.0	14.0	4,000	40.0
Primary Metals: ALCOA only	9.3	5.8	−3,500	−37.6
Nonelectrical Machinery	1.0	0.8	− 200	−20.0
Other durables[1]	2.8	2.9	100	3.6
Subtotal	(23.1)	(23.5)	(400)	1.7
Predominantly Local Service Industries				
Food	3.6	4.0	400	11.1
Printing and publishing	0.8	1.1	300	37.5
Stone, clay, and glass	1.7	1.8	100	5.9
Subtotal	(6.1)	(6.9)	(800)	−13.1
Other Nondurable Goods Industries[2]	1.4	1.1	−300	−21.4
Total Manufacturing	43.8	42.1	−1,700	− 3.9

Sources: Tennessee Department of Employment Security and others. Reproduced from Hammer and Company Associates, "The Economy of Metropolitan Knoxville," prepared for the Metropolitan Planning Commission of Knoxville and Knox County (Washington, D.C., 1962).

Note: Average annual employment figures.

[1] Other durables not elsewhere classified include: (*a*) primary metals, apart from ALCOA, (*b*) fabricated metals, (*c*) electrical machinery, (*d*) transportation equipment, (*e*) instruments, and (*f*) miscellaneous manufactures.

[2] Other nondurables not classified include: (*a*) chemicals—apart from the Oak Ridge operations of AEC, (*b*) tobacco, (*c*) paper, (*d*) petroleum, (*e*) rubber and plastics, and (*f*) leather products.

from 1,050 to 150. All to no avail. Brookside soon was forced to close, as was Appalachian Mills, which had been operating in Knoxville for forty-five years.[5]

Textile manufacturing was not the only industry in difficulty. The construction and lumber industries, after a wartime expansion, both suffered, the latter losing nearly 1,000 jobs in the 1950s. And newer industries that might have been expected to take up the slack simply were unable to do so. ALCOA had been a major employer in the region since its founding in 1928, having reached a peak of 9,300 employees in 1940. But by 1954 that figure had dropped to 7,800 and by 1960 to 5,800, a disastrous decline of 3,500 jobs. The end of the Korean war and (as the company explained) the "stretching out of the defense program" had left ALCOA with enormous aluminum stockpiles and declining orders, and the company could survive only if it drastically slashed employment. Similarly, AEC enterprises at nearby Oak Ridge no longer needed construction workers, and AEC employment in Oak Ridge during the 1950s declined by around 9,500 jobs. The economic consequences of this drop were felt throughout the metropolitan area.[6]

Some sectors of the local economy did grow, notably the service sector, the apparel industry, and the University of Tennessee. Indeed, all the city's leading growth industries were service producers or nondurable goods manufacturers (notably, apparel). UT alone gained 1,600 jobs between 1948 and 1960, while the apparel industry added approximately 1,200 new jobs. But the better-paying positions at UT usually went to newcomers from outside the region and not to those thrown out of work by the decline of other local industries. For its part, the apparel industry did grow, expanding existing facilities and adding new mills. One firm established itself in a mill vacated by a textile firm. But most of these new jobs went to females who worked for low wages, wages often rationalized by the assertion that these women were the "second breadwinners" in their families. Given the bleak employment picture, however, it is reasonable to assume that many were not.[7]

[5] Hammer report, 35, table 16; see *News-Sentinel*, Jan. 1, 1954; Jan. 19, 1954; Feb. 10, 1954; June 5, 1954; and Mar. 12, 1956, for specifics on mill closings in Knoxville and their impact.

[6] Hammer report, 29, and table 14, p. 36, and table 16; for aluminum stockpiles, see *News-Sentinel*, Jan. 1, 1954.

[7] For apparel industry new jobs, see Hammer report, 35. The apparel industry between 1960 and 1967 accounted for 3,500 of the 5,300-job employment increase. But while in the nation jobs paying less than $5,000 annually grew by only 10% they grew by 30% in the 201-county TVA region, and by 60% in the Knox County and Knoxville SMSA. See also Real Estate Research Corporation (RERC), *Trends, Conditions and Forecasts of Knoxville's Economy and the Potential Demand for Land and Structures*, prepared for the Community improvement Program, Knoxville Metropolitan Planning Commission (June 1969), 42, 43, 53. For national trends on women in the labor force, in which married women went from 36% in 1940 to 52% in 1950, see *America's Working Women: A Documentary History—1600 to the Present*, ed.

Unemployment figures for Knoxville make it clear that the "affluent society" did not include everyone. The percentage of Knoxvillians unemployed, consistently above the national average, rose from 5.8 percent in 1951 to a disturbing 9.7 percent in 1958. Yet these percentages reflect only those unemployed persons who remained in the city. As we shall see, a number vacated Knoxville in search of opportunities elsewhere. Had these men and women been included, Knoxville's unemployment statistics would have been truly staggering. Moreover, the jobs that were available at UT, Oak Ridge, or TVA (which itself lost 400 jobs between 1948 and 1960) were ones for which few of these people could qualify. In a characteristic understatement of the situation, one report blandly noted, "It is believed that a very high proportion of the unemployed do not have skills which are usable in today's market."[8]

With unemployment high and with many of the new jobs (in the apparel industry, for example) paying low wages, it is not surprising that real per capita income failed to grow significantly. Between 1950 and 1960 the real per capita income of the metropolitan area (comprising the counties of Knox, Anderson, and Blount) grew an anemic 16.7 percent (from $1,381 to $1,612)—4.7 percent behind Chattanooga, 5.8 percent behind Nashville, 3.8 percent behind Tennessee, and 5.7 percent behind the Southeast. Worse, the metro Knoxville figures are misleading, badly skewed by Anderson County's (Oak Ridge) increase of 64.4 percent. Indeed, Knox County alone had a real per capita income increase of but 9.1 percent, not even enough to match the modest national inflation rate of the 1950s. Moreover, it can be supposed that Knoxville city's per capita increase (figures are not available) was even more meager, for the city contained the highest proportion of people earning under $3,000 of all metropolitan areas in Tennessee.[9]

The closings of the Brookside Mills and Appalachian Mills in 1956–1957 shocked many Knoxvillians and threw the city council into a characteristic

---

Rosalyn Baxendall, Linda Gordon, and Susan Reverby (New York, 1976), appendix, "The Female Labor Force," 405.

[8]Hammer report, 91–92, and table 34. While between 4 and 6% unemployed indicates a "condition of labor surplus," a rate of more than 6% indicates "structural unemployment." Between 1951 and 1960, while the U.S. averaged 4.6% of the civilian labor force unemployed, metro Knoxville's average unemployment was 6.5% or 9,600 workers. Ibid., 91–92. Losses in construction employment at Oak Ridge were striking. The net loss between 1948 and 1960 was only 400 jobs, but construction work went from 11,200 jobs in 1954 to 1,700 jobs in 1960. The low net loss is owing to the fact that in 1948 only 2,100 were employed in construction. Overall, Oak Ridge lost 3,500 jobs in the period between 1948 and 1960. Ibid., 29 and table 14.

[9]Hammer report, 100, table 37. The City of Knoxville in 1959 had 33% of its population earning under $3,000; 27% between $3,000 and $4,999; 32% from $5,000 to $9,999; and 8% $10,000 and over. For the same categories, the percentages in Oak Ridge were 7%, 10%, 56% and 27% and for Alcoa-Maryville, 27%, 20%, 43%, and 12%. Of the U.S. population, 15% was earning under $3,000.

panic. To many both on and off the council, the solution seemed to be to attract new industries to offset declines in textiles and other areas. But that was easier said than done. Noting that Knoxville had been successful in attracting some small firms but had let the large ones slip through its fingers, Councilman Roy H. Bass, Jr., in 1957 proposed establishing an industrial commission to promote Knoxville to industries looking for new sites.

Local AFL–CIO head Paul Christopher agreed, called Bass's proposal "one of the best things I have seen yet." At the same time, however, Christopher warned that some interests in Knoxville would be less than enthusiastic about attracting new industries. "The reputation that has been established here," Christopher said, "is enough to disinterest any industry that might be thinking of moving here." In fact, he argued, many in Knoxville paid only the barest lip service to luring new industries that paid higher wages, "only being interested in [the] sweatshop needle trades industry that pays one dollar an hour." The actual shifts in "old line" industrial employment would seem to support Christopher's argument since the needle trades (apparel industry) were the only "old line" manufacturing sector to grow in the metro economy (by 1,200 jobs, or 41 percent).

Replying to the labor leader's accusations, the *News-Sentinel* warmly disagreed with both Christopher and Bass, asserting that the Chamber of Commerce's Committee of 100 was already trying to attract new industries, was not being subverted by the business community, and should not be "interfered with" by a proposed industrial commission backed by the city council. "We are vigorously opposed," the *News-Sentinel* stated loftily, "to any deal between the city and a new industry whereby the latter receives special favors. . . . We don't think such deals are fair to already-established businesses."[10]

Whether the *News-Sentinel* unwittingly proved Christopher's charges is a moot point. What is clear is that Bass was right when he asserted that Knoxville had failed to attract enough new industries to offset job declines. Moreover, Bass had merely proposed the kind of effort (which was ultimately shelved) that other American cities, confronting problems like Knoxville's, were making. To save themselves, some cities were directly subsidizing industries by offering assistance in site selection, free sites, and alluring tax breaks similar to the one offered to Brookside Mills. Some cities had gone so far as to establish industrial parks with utilities, parking space, good transportation access, and pleasant atmosphere. By 1960 Birmingham had six such parks, Atlanta nine, Louisville eleven, Charlotte ten, Dallas twenty-one, and Memphis eight. Indeed, in the postwar battle for urban survival those cities that would triumph would be those that were most

[10]*News-Sentinel*, Jan. 3, 1957.

aggressive and innovative and those least shackled by the ideology of the past.[11]

But in Knoxville, rugged topography, which limited the amount of land suitable for industrial site development, was supplemented by rugged individualism. In 1960, when unemployment was high, a major industry approached Knoxville and inquired about building a large facility in the city. Predictably, site selection was a major stumbling block, and the industry had been offered beneficial site arrangements elsewhere. For his part, Knoxville's Mayor John Duncan was willing to offer the company a prepared site. He explained, "It may not be 100 percent right to subsidize industry, but it is 100 percent wrong to see men out of work and do nothing about it." Ignoring warnings, Duncan pushed ahead with a bond referendum for an industrial site development, "confident that all were in agreement on it." One can imagine his surprise and dismay when the Chamber of Commerce, unwilling to create "a state of affairs in which they paid taxes to subsidize a competitor for the local labor force," refused to support the proposal. By 1960 Knoxville had but one small "industrial park," which one report labeled "totally insufficient."[12]

By 1961 the disastrous decline in jobs and the failure to attract new industries had made some Knoxvillians almost frantic. From 1956 to 1961, thirty-five separate firms had expressed interest in locating in Knoxville. Over 75 percent of those enterprises were "new line" industries (electronics, chemicals, fabricated metals), especially prized because they were clean and paid high wages. The new industrial prospects planned to employ a total of 10,300 people. Yet ultimately none of the firms chose Knoxville. Several selected instead less urbanized locations along the Great Valley of East Tennessee. Hence, while Knoxville was experiencing serious economic deterioration, the East Tennessee region had added over 13,000 new jobs, 6,900 of them in "new line" industries. Although one Knoxville banker remarked in the 1950s that "anything that happens within 250 miles of here is good for Knoxville," undoubtedly he prayed fervently that the wish would be father to the deed.[13]

In desperation, the city council hired the Washington, DC, consulting firm of Hammer and Associates to investigate why so many opportunities had slipped through the city's hopeful fingers. A model of the intelligent uses to which regional history, demography, and economic statistics can be put, the Hammer report, entitled *The Economy of Metropolitan Knoxville,*

[11]David Dickey, Director, Industrial Development, Knoxville Chamber of Commerce, "Preliminary Recommendations for the 1960 Industrial Development Program," Metropolitan Planning Commission, Industrial Sites file, Knoxville.

[12]Baker, "Politics of Innovation," 71.

[13]Ibid., 70. On firms rejecting Knoxville see Hammer report, 154–57 and table 43.

should have surprised no one. It found that, of those firms that had rejected Knoxville between 1956 and 1961, 62 percent cited as their reason "cost, availability, or other features of industrial sites or buildings. . . . [A]t present there is an acute shortage of desirable sites for new manufacturing and related types of industry." Even though some firms added that lack of easy highway access and an insufficiently skilled labor pool also contributed to their decisions to go elsewhere, Hammer and Associates concluded that "industrial land appears to have been the main obstacle to the location of these industries in metropolitan Knoxville." And while the Washington consulting firm argued forcefully for a "major program of site acquisition and development" in order to prevent Knoxville's economic problems from becoming more "acute" in the future, at the same time Hammer and Associates feared that any such plans might be "too little too late."[14]

Three years later, in 1965, Charles H. Dean, KUB executive and chairman of the Chamber of Commerce's Industrial Sites Committee, reported in frustration that almost no progress had been made in site preparation. No fewer than four studies (the last being that of Hammer and Associates, which urged "immediate action") had reached the same conclusion, and three sites for industrial parks had actually been studied and recommended. Yet virtually no action had been taken in buying land and preparing sites. "In spite of the many surveys . . .," wrote Dean, "responsible leadership in this community (which is also the Chamber membership) has not seen fit to push the acquisition and development of medium and large industrial sites." In ill-disguised irritation, Dean pointed out, "If local authorities and/or private interests had used an amount of money comparable to that spent on the Coliseum to reserve land, we would be in pretty good shape today." Yet, it was clear that Knoxville was in anything but good shape. And, however sensitive the Chamber of Commerce and local business interests might have been about the issue of subsidization in one form or another, after numerous studies and Dean's blunt report they could hardly have been unaware of the potential consequences of their inaction.[15]

Not surprisingly, the severe economic dislocations of the 1950s directly

[14]Hammer report, 214, 231–33, 154–57, and table 43.

[15]C.H. Dean to the Industrial Council, Greater Knoxville Chamber of Commerce, June 30, 1965, Knoxville Metropolitan Planning Commission, Industrial Sites file. The studies were as follows: The Colonna and Pate Knoxville–Knox County Industrial Sites Survey (Sept. 1957), the MPC "Knox County Industrial Land Needs" Study (Sept. 1959), the Knoxville Chamber of Commerce Committee of 100, sites committee, "Sites for Industry Study" (Sept. 1959), and Chamber of Commerce staff study (May 1960). As to consequences, the U.S. Chamber of Commerce estimated during this period that for every 100 new factory jobs there were 359 more people, 91 more school children, 100 more households, 97 more passenger cars, 65 non-manufacturing jobs, 3 more retail establishments, and $710,000 more personal income per year with $331,000 more retail sales per year (Knoxville MPC, Industrial Sites Committee file).

affected population shifts. Between 1950 and 1960, the city population actually declined, from 124,183 to 111,800. If natural increase for the decade is taken into account, it can be seen that out-migration significantly exceeded the 12,383 loss between the two censuses. Indeed, since the entire metropolitan area (Knox, Anderson, and Blount counties) lost approximately 30,600 people to out-migration, it is reasonable to assume that *at least half* of these out-migrations were abandoning the city of Knoxville. The State Planning Commission reported that 12.2 percent of all Tennessee's out-migrants came from Knoxville. Over half of those left the state entirely, emigrating to Florida, Ohio, Georgia, California, Virginia, Alabama, and North Carolina, where job opportunities were rumored to be more abundant. According to the 1962 Hammer report, "There are few metropolitan areas in the U.S. for which a sharper decline in population growth—between two consecutive decades—has been recorded."[16]

Even more disturbing were the facts about who was leaving the city. An enormous proportion of the out-migrants were men and women between the ages of twenty-five and forty-four, the so-called productive group that traditionally is more fully employed, upwardly mobile, and consumer-oriented (purchasing homes, automobiles, furniture, adult and children's clothing), and that pays a comparatively high proportion of taxes. Between 1950 and 1960 Knoxville lost roughly 12,000 people from that group, as its share of the city's total population dropped from 31.6 percent in 1950 to 24.4 percent in 1960. "The simple reason for this shift," bemoaned the Hammer report,". . . was a sharp drop in the number of employment opportunities within metropolitan Knoxville during the 1950–1960 period."[17] Table 2 contains comparative rates of unemployment.

But if the declining job market was the chief reason for this rather substantial out-migration, then how many jobs would have been necessary to stanch the flow? This is precisely the question that concerned members of the civic-commercial elite began to ask themselves—although not until somewhat later. As the Hammer report stated, between 1950 and 1960 the Knoxville metropolitan area added approximately 12,000 new jobs. But those jobs, the report explained, could support a population gain of only about

[16] Hammer report, 62, 67, and table 26; *Population in Tennessee*, State Planning Division, Tennessee State Planning Commission, Publication no. 376 (Apr. 1970), 12, and table 6. Knoxville had the dubious distinction of being the only metro area in Tennessee that lost population to *all* other state metro areas. Ibid., 15.

[17] Hammer report, 62–63. The report indicated that between 1940 and 1960 the under-18 age group grew from 34.5% of the total population to 36.2%. The 65-and-over age group also increased its proportion from 5.1% in 1940 to 7.4% in 1960. Conversely, the working-age population fell from 60.3% to 56.4%. The economy therefore had to support a greater number of people who did not contribute as much as the working-age group (67 and table 26). For the age group 25 to 44, see RERC, "Trends," 31.

TABLE 2. *Rates of Unemployment, Metropolitan Knoxville
and Other Selected Areas 1951–60*

	KNOXVILLE	CHATTANOOGA	NASHVILLE	CHICAGO	DETROIT	WASHINGTON
1951	5.8%	4.7%	3.8%	2.5%	6.5%	2.5%
1952	5.2	4.7	4.5	2.4	1.3	2.4
1953	4.9	4.4	3.3	1.9	1.3	2.8
1954	7.4	7.7	5.5	5.4	5.5	3.1
1955	6.8	5.7	4.5	3.8	2.9	2.1
1956	6.8	5.6	4.4	2.4	5.4	1.9
1957	7.0	5.8	4.7	3.1	8.8	2.4
1958	9.7	7.9	5.9	7.3	16.5	2.8
1959	5.9	6.5	4.6	4.7	10.5	2.6
1960	6.2	6.3	4.1	4.3	7.6	2.6
10-year average	(6.5%)	(5.9%)	(4.5%)	(3.8%)	(7.0%)	(2.5%)

Sources: Tennessee Department of Employment Security, and Bureau of Employment Security, U.S. Department of Labor. Reproduced from Hammer and Company Associates, "The Economy of Metropolitan Knoxville," prepared for the Metropolitan Planning Commission of Knoxville and Knox County (Washington, D.C., 1962).

31,000 people. Since the metropolitan area's births exceeded deaths by about 61,000 during the decade of the now-famous "baby boom," *another* 12,000 jobs would have been required to stop the out-migration. And, as we have already seen, Knoxville lost the opportunity to attract industries that already had inquired about locating or relocating in the city and that could have provided more than 10,000 of the required employment positions.[18]

Hence, Knoxville's people were being propelled from their homes by dual forces—the American dream of economic success and upward mobility and the American nightmare of economic failure in the face of unemployment and lost job opportunities. Few desirable areas for residential development remained within the city limits, and interstate highway construction, expansion of the University of Tennessee, urban renewal and rezoning from residential to commercial all caused families to leave. It might also be mentioned that the city's housing stock was generally poor and worn out, and it was not easily convertible through the process of "gentrification," a point noticed less in the 1950s during the rush to the suburbs than in the late 1970s when many began to find life on the "crabgrass frontier"

[18]Hammer report, 64. Noting the moving up of natural increase rates, the report summed up: "increasing demands have therefore been on the metropolitan economy to provide support for people who were born and raised locally. Clearly the economy has been unable to satisfy these increasing demands for jobs." Ibid., 64.

less appealing than life on the new urban frontier. Much of Knoxville's housing stock from the industrial era was the extremely adaptable but somewhat insubstantial shotgun house.[19]

Whatever reasons people had for migrating out of the city proper, they left behind a population more static and disproportionately old, black, poor, unskilled, poorly housed, and badly in need of municipal, state, and federal services than they were. Between 1950 and 1960 Knoxville's "dependent" population (those under eighteen and over sixty-five) represented an astounding 80 percent of the city's population gain, as opposed to 30 percent during the previous decade. Indeed, the city had 2,400 more people over sixty-five in 1960 (9.5 percent of Knoxville's population) than it had had a decade before. Such demographic shifts, notes urbanist Howard Chudacoff, in most cities give rise to other problems: "poverty, crime, pollution, unemployment—faced with decaying physical plants and shrinking revenue bases." Had he added "increasingly shaky retail trade," Chudacoff would have been describing Knoxville itself.[20]

KNOXVILLE ON THE CRABGRASS FRONTIER

At the same time that the city proper was losing jobs and people, Knoxville was beginning to feel the national trend toward suburbanization, a trend that further separated Knoxvillians by class and race. Although suburbanization would not become massive until the 1960s, in the 1950s the bedroom communities just outside the city's 1917 limits grew faster than any component in the entire metropolitan area. They gained approximately 37,500 persons between 1950 and 1960, an astonishing increase of 160.3 percent. By 1960 Knoxville had 111,800 people, while the county outside the city had 138,700, mostly concentrated on the city's fringe.[21]

During the 1950s suburban growth was generally symmetrical, and developments blossomed on all sides of the city's fringe. Along Chapman Highway suburban development produced a 32-percent population increase; to the east, Burlington grew by 47 percent; along Kingston Pike to the west (the scene of the most massive suburbanization in the 1960s and 1970s)

[19] Aelred J. Gray and Susan F. Adams, "Government," in Deaderick, ed., *Heart of the Valley*, 124. This particular chapter, the most outstanding in the work, provides a superb analysis of Knoxville from a planner's perspective.

[20] On Knoxville age groups and their proportionate growth, see RERC, "Trends," 33. For national trends, see Chudacoff, *Evolution*, 263.

[21] Hammer report, 77. Another study by Hammer stated prophetically in 1955 that "if Knoxville's city limits are not expanded, there will be more Knox County people in the areas outside Knoxville than in Knoxville in 1960—for the first time since frontier days" (Hammer and Company Associates, "Knoxville's CBD" [Atlanta, 1955], copy in MPC files).

developments off Sutherland Avenue and south of Kingston Pike accounted for a 38-percent population increase. To the north, Fountain City's growth had been impressive. A small community since the late eighteenth century, Fountain City had become something of a vacation spot for Knoxvillians and ultimately the site of impressive residential dwellings. Now people rushed to fill in the available land, and the population of the once-peaceful community soared from 5,000 in 1930 to roughly 20,000 by 1960. Planners expected Fountain City ultimately to grow to about 35,000 people.[22]

As in other cities in the 1950s, suburbanization in Knoxville was spurred by upward mobility, the triumph of the automobile, the increasing ease of obtaining mortgages and credit, and the growth in capacity of public utilities. Between 1945 and 1950, U.S. automobile registrations jumped from 25 million to over 40 million and by the mid-1950s were approaching 50 million. Almost immediately, highway access and automobiles facilitated the movement to the suburbs. Notes Howard Chudacoff, "Thus outward movement energized a new multiplier effect. Access to highways attracted residents, who in turn lured businesses, who then brought jobs and more enticement for residential development." In metropolitan Knoxville automobile registrations increased from roughly 64,100 in 1948 to 74,800 in 1950 and an astounding 107,600 in 1954, almost equaling national per capita average increases.[23]

Simultaneously with growing automobility, FHA mortgage insurance and Veterans' Administration loans "virtually eliminated down payments, enabling lower middle class families and even some working class families to buy or build in the urban outskirts. The ease of credit and the acceleration of general prosperity by the late 1940s triggered a massive construction boom that lasted for nearly a decade." Moreover, in 1956, when a state statute prohibiting the establishment of new utility districts was repealed, six new districts were almost immediately created around Knoxville, further spurring suburban development. Indeed, in the thirteen years that the statute had been on the books (1943–1956) suburbanization had continued despite the lack of public utilities, with fifty-six new subdivisions built in those years. Residents simply resorted to wells and septic tanks and depended on KUB for electricity, on private companies for garbage collection and fire protection,

---

[22]Hammer, "Knoxville's CBD, 6; Deaderick, ed., *Heart of the Valley*, 125; Larry Smith and Company, Real Estate Consultants, "Market Square Development Feasibility Study," Nov. 30, 1960 (copy in MPC files), 8.

[23]Chudacoff, *Evolution*, 264, 266, 268. Chudacoff notes "that in 1950 alone almost a million single-family houses were begun, the vast majority of which sprouted in outlying or suburban districts." Ibid., 265. For Knoxville automobile registrations, see Hammer, "Knoxville's CBD," table 9, p. 41.

and on a severely understaffed county sheriff's department for safety and order.[24]

Although permitting development in advance of the installation of public utilities and services was certainly a popular decision in the mid-1950s (and even into the early 1970s, when a Metropolitan Planning Commission's ruling of "no sewers, no subdivision" would be opposed vehemently by developers and would-be suburbanites), it was a decision for which Knoxvillians would pay dearly. In 1962, when a desperate city government at last would annex these suburbs to shore up its deteriorating tax base, it would discover that most of these subdivisions had roads with no curbs, gutters, or storm sewers and that a number of them had no sewers at all. The cost of providing sewers alone would be in excess of $40 million.[25]

In truth, suburbanization was an almost irresistible trend. By 1970 more Americans were living in suburbs than in cities, a reality that Knoxville barely sidestepped by its massive 1962 annexation of northern and western suburbs. Moreover, those who came to reside in suburbs were generally the more affluent citizens, for whom suburbanization became an entire way of life complete with its own value structure, lifestyles for men and women, criteria for success, and social problems.

Illustrative of this new way of life was Knoxville's 1954 Parade of Homes, which featured the new West Hills subdivision, located north of Kingston Pike between the city limits and the Bearden area. That year the Parade was graced by the presence of the 1954 Mrs. America, Wanda Jennings, a "prize-winning pumpkin pie baker" who dodged sunlight "because it makes me freckle." Mrs. America chortled that her husband would "be aghast when I tell him what I want after seeing your parade of homes." Her preferences were for a "pushbutton music system," floor-length windows, and a patio "shaded over in light green plastic"—the latter presumably to keep nature at a tasteful distance and preserve skin tone. The early 1950s envisioned a suburban Eden where the serpent of moral relativism had not yet intruded. Mrs. America not only knew what the happy home should look like, but how to preserve it: "Treat your family like honored guests and take your domestic problems to your family pastor."

The 1956 Parade of Homes in Fountain City's Sherwood Forest subdivision stressed the escape from urban life by advertising "a new way of living" rather than merely a house. With the verbal overkill so characteristic of mass marketing, the advertisement emphasized the three living areas of the house: family room, screened porch, and terrace for relaxation; living room for entertaining; and "playroom space in the basement for fun!" In Westhaven

[24]Chudacoff, *Evolution*, 264–66, 269; Deaderick, ed., *Heart of the Valley*, 125.
[25]Deaderick, ed., *Heart of the Valley*, 125.

Village, young suburbanites were attracted to "ultramodern three bedroom, 1½ baths, family room, living room, terrace" at 1,196 square feet for $700 down on the GI bill, $89.70 per month. Obviously, the new way of life had the old in complete rout, and memories of the Great Depression dimmed in the easy-credit, television-oriented, materialistic culture of the suburbs. For the *News-Sentinel*, one word was enough to describe the lure of suburbanization:"ROMANCE."[26] Noting the market for suburban homes, the *News-Sentinel* predicted that the "economic outlook for 1970" would be "many two-house families" with houses in the $14,000 to $30,000 range.[27]

As affluence moved to the suburbs, retail establishments, eager to capitalize on the young homeowners market, followed. In fact, they pursued this market to such a degree that placement of shopping centers in the 1950s exceeded the need. By 1960 there were ten "significant" suburban retailing operations in Knoxville with an annual sales potential of nearly $15 million each, ranging from small (23,000 square feet) to large (114,000 square feet). These were heavily concentrated to the north and west, and all had been built in the 1950s. The suburbs' massive orientation to the automobile made parking space a singular feature of the new shopping centers. The Fountain City Shopping Center on North Broadway boasted "off-street parking for 200," while Broadway Shopping Center, advertising its location ("2½ miles from Knoxville, near Fountain City") and its potential market ("32,000 people reside within a one-mile radius") drawing upon Park City, Oakwood, and Lincoln Park suburbs, offered parking for 750 cars. Announcement of a shopping center near Merchants Road, to be anchored by a Winn-Dixie food store and S.S. Kresge, projected parking spaces for 1,500 cars. And nearby Norwood Shopping Center, located in the midst of a suburb created out of nursery land after World War II, boasted 2,000 parking spaces. As churches, schools, and social organizations for parents and children were founded along with these retail shopping centers, suburbanites found fewer and fewer reasons to go to downtown Knoxville at all.[28]

THE INNER CITY FIGHTS BACK

What greeted those suburbanites who did venture downtown was a deteriorating city with poor automobile access, limited parking, smoke and coal ash, and growing slums. Designed and developed before the impact of the automobile made itself felt, Knoxville seemed to be a city frozen in time,

---

[26] *News-Sentinel*, Sept. 17, 18, and 19, 1954.

[27] Ibid., Aug. 17, 1958, Sept. 16, 1956.

[28] Larry Smith and Company, "Market Square," 8; *News-Sentinel*, May 18, 1954; Sept. 19 and 20, 1956; Feb. 7, 1959, and Apr. 26, 1959.

out of touch with the rapidly changing world. True, the coming of TVA and electric power, the conversion of coal-fired locomotives to diesel, and the removal of the Coster roundhouse out to the John Sevier yards had improved the look of the city. But it was still dirty. The *News-Sentinel* exulted in 1950 that the 1949 sootfall had fallen to a record low of 143.3 tons of dust and soot per square mile, the record high of 1930 had been 348.6 tons.[29]

Much of the city was unsightly, if for no other reason than its age. Vine and Jackson, Buffalo Alley, Willow Avenue, the riverfront, First Creek Valley, Morningside Heights, McAnnaly Flats, old Holston Hill, Mechanicsville, Brookside Village, to name but some neighborhoods, were remnants of an older, industrial Knoxville. In 1954 a program called Operation Facelift attempted slum improvement in a pilot block bounded by West Fifth Avenue, University Avenue, and Arthur, Douglas, and Calloway streets (Mechanicsville). The project chairman, Cliff Greenwood, stated the need for such programs in the city: "The lack of a workable program of blight prevention has resulted in 85 percent of the in-city area being blacklisted for FHA loans for new construction." Yet the pilot project was extremely modest and did not seem to encourage others to follow. Knoxville was unattractive to suburbanites and slow to change.[30]

Worse, automobile access to the downtown itself was severely limited. Once the suburbanite had successfully if slowly negotiated one of the many bottlenecks, he or she confronted jammed streets and a dearth of parking. Between 1948 and 1955, there was a 32-percent increase in vehicular volume, while the number of passengers riding the KTL buses declined 36 percent. On the eight major arteries into the city, the peak-hour load rose to 14,000 vehicles in 1955; yet the capacity of those access routes was only 9,900 vehicles. To better understand the problem, the city commissioned six separate traffic and street plan studies between 1945 and 1959, as if successive surveys might themselves solve the problem. But each study reached basically the same conclusion. As one (1955) put it: "Knoxville and other cities face a Hobson's choice when they concentrate on moving vehicles instead of people. . . . Knoxville has come to a crossroad. It has reached a point where its major downtown traffic gateways are operated at above capacity. Its major arterial system is several years (maybe more) from completion. In the meantime mounting downtown congestion can accelerate decentralization of downtown businesses."[31] Clogged access roads and other traffic problems discouraged the comparatively affluent suburbanites

[29]*News-Sentinel*, Jan. 16, 1950.

[30]Ibid., Oct. 10, 1954.

[31]Hammer, "Knoxville's CBD," 47–49. For effects of increased automotive registrations see ibid., 46. For successive street plan studies, see A.J. Gray, "Center City Major Studies and Project Proposals, 1930–1973," Report to the Center City Task Force (May 1974), copy in MPC

from coming downtown except to work. Small wonder that the *News-Sentinel*, urging repair of Western Avenue, the main artery into Knoxville from Oak Ridge, complained: the "condition of Western Avenue is so bad it discourages Oak Ridgers with the highest buying income in the state ($7,000 per year) from coming to Knoxville."[32]

Inadequate parking facilities further discouraged the would-be shopper. When the grossly insufficient number of legal parking spaces was filled, drivers blithely parked their automobiles wherever they chose. In anger and frustration, the *News-Sentinel* noted that "curb parking in no parking zones is one of the worst business deterrents in the downtown section, and is also a major cause of traffic jams." But when city safety director David Garrison, in a one-week "experiment," tried to enforce strictly parking regulations in the downtown core, businessmen were irate, complaining loudly that the overzealous Garrison was driving away shoppers. Watching another of its efforts fail, the *News-Sentinel* lamented weakly that "indiscriminate curbside parking in the retail shopping area ought to be ended; Knoxville is no crossroads village."[33]

Besides traffic flow and parking, there was another problem in the downtown core that disoriented shoppers. Recent students of shopping mall developments and downtown rejuvenation projects have come to believe that, in order to derive maximum benefits from pedestrian traffic in retail trade areas, those areas must be "anchored" by a number of very large and popular establishments such as Sears, J.C. Penney, and the like. These students see these "anchors" as both luring shoppers into these areas and, equally important, keeping them moving from one anchor to another, past smaller retail establishmenhs in between. These anchors, then, theoretically act to keep shoppers *inside* the designated trade areas; once shoppers pass beyond these anchors, they will rarely reenter the core areas to make purchases. For these reasons, shopping-center developers are extremely anxious to attract such anchoring establishments to their projects. Without these anchors, such projects are, at best, risky undertakings.

In 1950 Knoxville's downtown core was anchored by the S.H. George department store on the northeastern corner of Gay and Wall, and Miller's department store one block to the north, on the corner of Gay and Union. Across South Gay Street in this block were mainstays of downtown businesses, among them Spence's, Kimball's, Woodruff's, J.S. Hall's, and the Paul Dean department store. Between the two anchors on South Gay were the Strand Theater, Lerner's, Baker's, S.H. Kress, and McClellan's five-

---

files, 10. A 1948 major street-plan study indicated then that the "gateways" to Knoxville were operating at peak traffic flows. Even so, the report's 1970 traffic projections were achieved as early as 1955. Hammer, "Knoxville's CBD," 34, and Gray, "Center City Major Studies," 10.

[32]*News-Sentinel*, Mar. 4, 1956.

[33]Ibid., Feb. 7, 1959.

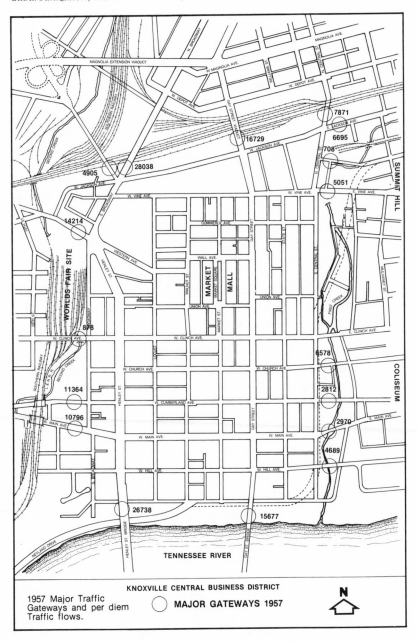

IV. Major Traffic Gateways, 1957

and-dime store. Behind South Gay between Wall and Union were shops fronting on Market Square and the Market House. As can be seen, the core area was very close-knit and was oriented to South Gay Street.[34]

Poor access to the core and congestion within its streets prompted some retailers to take matters into their own hands. In doing so, however, they unwittingly violated the anchor theory, with unfortunate results. In 1952 Rich's of Atlanta purchased S.H. George's, and in 1954 Rich's announced its plans to build a new store on a different site. This site, "within walking distance of the very center of the city and yet far enough away to be out of the terrible congestion of Gay Street," was on the Henley, Clinch, Locust, and Church block. Planned to incorporate a "quick service" parking garage with space for 1,500 cars, the new building replaced some familiar landmarks—the lighthouse service station on Clinch and Locust, the "whitebrick" doctors' offices on Church, and the Kincaid Apartments.[35]

The relocation of one of the principal anchors of the central business district (CBD) was disorienting: "This location had a disastrous effect on the established shopping patterns of the CBD by creating a strong attraction three blocks west and three blocks south. Land values dropped in the north end of the CBD. Specialty shops had a difficult time surviving as they searched for suitable locations without clearly defined shopper traffic." To further refocus the CBD, the other anchor, Miller's, purchased the old Colonial Hotel block, which was bounded by Gay, State, Cumberland, and Main, and extended north from the Lyric Theater and Louis' Steak House. That move never took place, because Rich's soon left Knoxville. Then, Miller's moved to the Rich's building on the Henley Street block. But had it been completed, Miller's new store would have reoriented the CBD in the same way that the new United American Bank building, constructed in 1977–1978, now anchors the south and east of the CBD.[36]

Indeed, the problems of suburbanization, automobility, and the deterioration of the downtown, both physically and as a retail shopping core, seemed almost insurmountable. Were all that not enough, the Interstate Highway Act (1956) threatened to accelerate suburbanization and place those more affluent residential developments farther and farther from the downtown core. Downtown retailers were plainly worried; if they had not been able even to firmly situate their anchors and preserve their own core, how could they hope to prevent wholesale desertion by retailers following their more well-to-do customers into the new suburbs? Up to the mid-1950s, one study

[34] Hammer, "Knoxville's CBD," downtown map.

[35] On the announcement of Rich's, see *News-Sentinel*, Jan. 18, 1954. For location of the removed buildings and accompanying photographs, see ibid., Mar. 7, 1954.

[36] Deaderick, ed., *Heart of the Valley*, 130–31; *News-Sentinel*, June 2, 1954. The proposed move of Miller's also stressed parking facilities, projecting "the largest under one roof in Tennessee," which would service "2,000 to 2,500 cars daily."

showed, Knoxville's suburbanization had been fairly symmetrical, moving out in an almost even radius from the downtown core. This fact gave many downtown merchants hope. However, interstate highway construction obviously would destroy that symmetry. Clearly, the time had come to act or die.[37]

As early as 1954 many believed inadequate parking to be the downtown's key problem. City engineer Robert Stuart underlined this belief, calling downtown traffic and parking problems "pressing and complex." In 1954 Mayor George Dempster proposed a truly bizarre solution to the parking problem: he wanted a parking lot built on top of the Market House in the center city. This move, fortunately, was blocked by the original 1853 deed of Mabry and Swan, which forbade multiple uses for the building. Outrageous as it was, Dempster's scheme was the only one put forward to meet the crisis. Those who urged shoppers to use city buses ignored the fact that use of bus transportation had been declining since the late 1940s.[38]

Others saw poor access to the downtown core as the central issue. Mayor Jack Dance, Dempster's successor, pushed for the long-overdue creation of a Metropolitan Planning Commission (MPC) and the development of a "downtown loop." The plan, conceived by the first MPC director, Joe Whitlow, called for "a four or six lane limited access highway from Kingston Pike along Neyland Drive lakefront route, up First Creek Valley, connecting with the east Knoxville interregional expressway." The goal was to improve access from West Knoxville by circumventing the congested Cumberland-Main area and linking up with the proposed interstate highway, and to improve access from the east and northeast by overcoming the topographical barrier of First Creek Valley. Planning was completed by 1957, though the east leg was not constructed until the late 1960s and the remainder of the route not until the mid-1970s. Even so, a step toward improving access had been taken and a great incentive provided for urban renewal along the new loop and for later location of the coliseum-auditorium across First Creek Valley.[39]

[37] Hammer, "Knoxville's CBD," 7. "The uniformity of suburban growth in Knox County is of particular importance to the Central Business District. . . . From their central position the retail facilities of downtown Knoxville are in a good position to reach the expanding markets that are growing outward in all directions." Ibid.

[38] *News-Sentinel*, July 4, 1954.

[39] On the importance of Mayor Dance and Joe B. Whitlow to development of the downtown loop, see Deaderick, ed., *Heart of the Valley*, 129–30, and Gray, "Center City Major Studies," 11. In many respects the development of the loop was mutually interactive with redevelopment proposals. The mayor returned to the idea of a coliseum-auditorium in the Riverfront–Willow Avenue redevelopment area as increased pressure was put on the state to approve the loop highway in First Creek Valley. *News-Sentinel*, Feb. 22, 1957. However, the Clinch Avenue Bridge across First Creek, part of the redevelopment project, was rendered "probably . . . useless" with the completion of the loop. Ibid., Feb. 11, 1959.

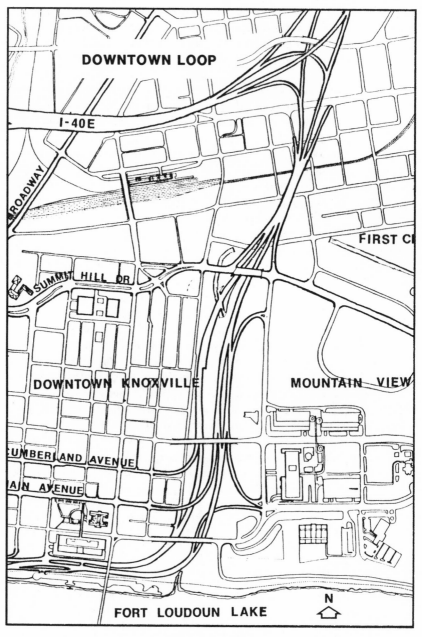

V. Downtown Loop

Dance did not live to see his dreams realized. Had he done so, he might well have been frustrated by the slow pace at which his plans bore fruit. When Dance died unexpectedly in office, his term was filled by the caretaker administration of obstructionist Vice-Mayor Cas Walker. Commenting on the Dance administration's urban renewal program in an editorial on May 6, 1959, the *Journal* was of the opinion that his efforts were "in line with efforts to combat suburbia" and cited "experts" who predicted that people would drift back from the suburbs "sadder but wiser," disillusioned by sewerage and garbage disposal problems and by "chauffering children back and forth." Indeed, the "experts" were not wrong, just several decades premature.[40]

The central question was whether downtown Knoxville would deteriorate and collapse completely before Dance's plans could take effect. Suburbanization was increasing at such a rapid rate that county mail carriers were swamped, necessitating the extension of city mail delivery beyond the city limits into the suburbs. Some downtown core retailers looked as if they were preparing to bolt for greener pastures, and others—Rich's in particular— seemed to be sinking. The anchors seemed to be drifting away, threatening to leave the downtown core anchorless and abandoned by both retailers and customers.

In 1956 businessmen formed the Downtown Knoxville Association (DKA) to mobilize planning for the CBD. The DKA was eventually to have its limited successes in reinvigorating downtown, but the problems of urban core disintegration demanded ambitious projects requiring infusion of money and planning activity beyond the scale attainable by the city's businessmen. With future profits precarious at best, and warily watching one another for the first signs of desertion to the suburbs, merchants understandably were unwilling to gamble everything on the slim prospect of rapid downtown rejuvenation. Another serious defect in the DKA's ability to effect a greater transformation was the plethora of proposals, including the imitation of the suburbs by the creation of a downtown "super shopping center," numerous plans to reanchor downtown in the vicinity of the new Rich's store on Henley Street, and even the creation of "moving sidewalks and pedestrian malls."[41]

It took no prophet to recognize, as most downtown businessmen did, that "something had to be done to maintain the downtown area," but agreement on what that "something" should be was hard to elicit.[42] Faced with a

---

[40]*Journal*, May 6, 1958.

[41]The "super shopping center" proposal was a *News-Sentinel*, July 31, 1958, editorial. Plans for responding to locational shifts in the CBD are discussed in Gray, "Center City Major Studies," 7.

[42]Baker, "Politics of Innovation," 68–69. As one respondent stated of downtown: "It was

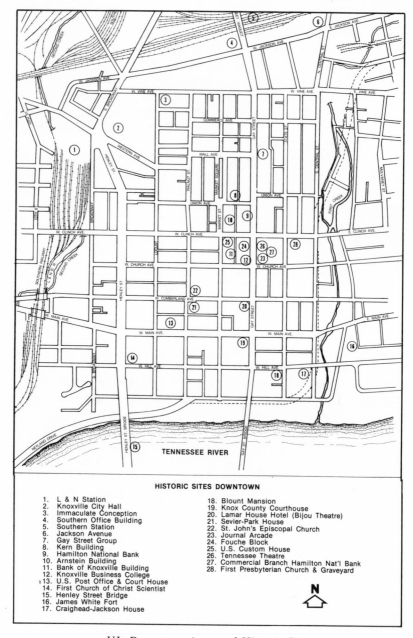

HISTORIC SITES DOWNTOWN

1. L & N Station
2. Knoxville City Hall
3. Immaculate Conception
4. Southern Office Building
5. Southern Station
6. Jackson Avenue
7. Gay Street Group
8. Kern Building
9. Hamilton National Bank
10. Arnstein Building
11. Bank of Knoxville Building
12. Knoxville Business College
13. U.S. Post Office & Court House
14. First Church of Christ Scientist
15. Henley Street Bridge
16. James White Fort
17. Craighead-Jackson House

18. Blount Mansion
19. Knox County Courthouse
20. Lamar House Hotel (Bijou Theatre)
21. Sevier-Park House
22. St. John's Episcopal Church
23. Journal Arcade
24. Fouche Block
25. U.S. Custom House
26. Tennessee Theatre
27. Commercial Branch Hamilton Nat'l Bank
28. First Presbyterian Church & Graveyard

N

VI. Downtown Area and Historic Sites

myriad of small plans and suggestions, and without the necessary financial supports and integral planning structure, Knoxville's businessmen preferred to undertake more modest cosmetic projects while disguising their vulnerable positions with an avalanche of press releases.

The first project undertaken by the DKA in its "bold new pattern of progress" was the Downtown Promenade and Parking Plaza, which, borrowing a concept from their suburban competitors, was billed as the "shopping center for East Tennessee." The Promenade was a private undertaking to refurbish the rear of the stores on the east side of Gay Street between Union and Wall. One brochure described the rears of these stores as an area of "old warehouses and unsightly alleys full of fire escapes and garbage cans." One hundred and thirty-three merchants were involved in this project, which was completed in March 1960 at a cost of $550 per linear foot, excluding remodeling. The rundown buildings behind the Gay Street stores were demolished and replaced with parking lots. These in turn were connected by an escalator (oddly called a "moving sidewalk ramp") to a new promenade along the rears of the stores, which became new store fronts with display space.[43]

Promenade introduced Knoxville to such renovative ideas as the "parking wall" concept and the "pedestrian way." DKA President J.W. Sullivan waxed lyrical about the 24-foot-wide Promenade, left roofless for one-half of its width so that "city workers and shoppers could sun themselves." The Promenade, said Sullivan, "would be a thing of beauty," enhancing functionality with graceful design by covering the rear of the stores to roof height with aluminum mesh to hide unsightly fire escapes and other eyesores. The promenade feature, Sullivan pointed out, was, "so far as we know . . . unique among American cities. . . . Uniform show windows at the rear of all stores" would display East Tennessee products "because the promenade will be a community project that will make all the people of East Tennessee want to come to Knoxville." Despite Hammer and Associates' warnings that public transit systems for people were more important than automobile movement in resolving downtown problems, the Promenade enshrined the very machines that were choking it. Trying to replicate in downtown the atmosphere of a suburban shopping center, the DKA ironically employed car-to-store "moving sidewalks" and a promenade "wide enough for all new models of automobiles to be shown when they are introduced."[44]

---

deteriorating and Knoxville was losing population. Something had to be done to make the downtown area into an attractive place to shop." Ibid., 69. On the extension of mail routes see *News-Sentinel*, Jan. 3, 1950.

[43] Metropolitan Planning Commission, "The Downtown Knoxville Story" (1965, MPC files). See also Gray, "Center City Major Studies," 4. The downtown merchants used a "joint venture agreement" which required 100% participation before individual agreements were in force. Ibid.

[44] Gray, "Center City Major Studies," 4; *News-Sentinel*, Feb. 1, 1959.

Old Market House

BECK CULTURAL EXCHANGE CENTER

When a fire destroyed the old Market House behind the core of the CBD in 1960, the DKA had another opportunity to enhance the appearance of downtown with the construction of a mall. The Market House area where the city's traditional central food market was located had been suggested as a possible mall site earlier, but it had been opposed by those who wished to preserve the Market House.[45]

The DKA approached Larry Smith and Associates, real estate consultants, about the feasibility of creating a "truly unique retail environment." Apparently the DKA was willing to demolish "all existing buildings in the Market Square Area." Smith and Associates, however, felt that the DKA "should continue to promote the upgrading of the Market Square area . . . through means other than large scale demolition and construction of new facilities." The analysts felt that construction of new facilities was not wise because of severe site limitations, that high rents would be necessary to cover costs, and that in 1960 the Knoxville market area was already "overbuilt in terms of retail facilities." The Smith report stressed that large retail anchors could not be brought in from outside because of site and design limitations and property costs, and that even if some of these problems could be overcome "we believe that the local tax situation in Knoxville would present cause for concern to any potential developer undertaking the Market Square Project." Because of the latter problem, Knoxvillians were "strongly" advised "to actively pursue the program of tax equalization which we now understand is underway."[46]

Indeed, Smith and Associates chided the DKA for being at once too visionary and too timid. As noted above, the report discouraged ambitious schemes for massive demolition and construction of new retail facilities on the Market House site. At the same time, it criticized downtown merchants for thinking only in the narrow terms of retail activity:

> Our study of Knoxville has indicated to us that the future of downtown Knoxville will increasingly depend on the downtown's becoming such a true metropolitan center. Retailing will always be important, but for a city of Knoxville's size, downtown functions will increasingly give consideration to office-using activities, convention facilities and the providing of cultural services for the entire region.[47]

Yet despite the Smith and Associates' emphasis on the necessity of Knoxville's becoming a "true metropolitan center" if it were to survive, the DKA continued to concentrate its attention on cosmetic changes designed to entice

---

[45] Gray, "Center City Major Studies," 4–5.

[46] Larry Smith and Company to the Downtown Knoxville Association, Inc., 302 Mercantile Building, Knoxville, Nov. 30, 1960 (MPC files), 2–3.

[47] Ibid., 3–4.

shoppers back to the downtown core. In this spirit, it proceeded to make the Market Square Mall a reality. The product of joint effort, the mall plan was prepared by the MPC, designed "as a public service" by the East Tennessee chapter of the American Institute of Architects, promoted by the DKA, and participated in by 142 property owners. Though planned as a "beautiful oasis" where "trees grow, flowers bloom, fountains splash, and people enjoy themselves in the heart of Downtown Knoxville," aesthetically the project was less than successful. It looked like a series of canopies masking dilapidated buildings. Yet in time the Market Square Mall did become something of an oasis, if not as magnificent as many had predicted. Later, in the 1970s, the building of the TVA towers at the north end of the mall provided the kind of "new anchor" that Smith and Associates had earlier recommended.

The mall project was the occasion for a confrontation between the proponents of the "old" Knoxville and those of the "new." Cas Walker had a store on the Market Square referred to by one writer as "a social center as well as a shopping area for the type of people referred to in Knoxville as 'country people' or 'Cas Walker voters' . . . in short, the Market Square was a symbol of the old Knoxville; an outlook and way of life which Cas Walker articulated and represented." Walker actively opposed the mall and threatened to move his store if the mall project was approved, a threat he eventually carried out.[48]

Perhaps the ultimate in cosmetic cures was the "Gay Way," a 1964 project that ultimately involved some 300 merchants. To trumpeting press releases that claimed that the Gay Way "rejuvenated two blocks of Knoxville's Main Street," the project was unveiled. "All overhanging permanent canopies were erected over new, wider sidewalks and a new modern lighting system was installed." But, after an initial flurry of excitement, shoppers returned to their previous ways. Worse, critics of the Gay Way proclaimed that too little natural light was admitted through the canopies, and one writer commented, "There are some problems at certain times because of the accumulation of automobile and bus exhaust fumes under the canopy." In sum, the DKA's much-ballyhooed projects generally were too modest to cause shoppers to alter their behavior patterns significantly. Though the downtown core looked a bit better physically, economically it was still in difficult straits.[49]

[48]MPC, "The Downtown Knoxville Story"; Gray, "Center City Major Studies," 5. Gray noted that the cost of the mall was $135,000, with the city paying for construction on the mall's center, the fountain, paving, open-air market covering, and the like, and the mall merchants paying for new storefronts and sidewalk canopies. On Walker and the mall, see Baker, "Politics of Innovation," 112.

[49]MPC, "The Downtown Knoxville Story"; Gray, "Center City Major Studies," 5. Cost to participating merchants was $150 a front foot.

Market Square Mall, Early 1960s

MCCLUNG HISTORICAL COLLECTION
KNOXVILLE–KNOX COUNTY PUBLIC LIBRARY

THE POLITICS OF PARALYSIS

It would be convenient to blame the continued troubles of Knoxville's core on downtown business people. After all, hadn't they ignored warnings about access and parking? Hadn't they overlooked Smith and Associates' desperate pleas to refocus their thinking? Hadn't they more than once broken ranks and fled to the more opulent suburbs? Hadn't they embraced cosmetic solutions rather than thinking boldly? Yet, while each of these questions holds a kernel of truth, it would be unfair to heap the blame solely on this harried group. Hindsight allows us to see what many failed to recognize at the time—that throughout the nation demographic, economic, and technological forces were at work that were so strong that they would have overpowered even the most imaginative efforts. In the mid-1950s it was by no means clear whether these forces were to be permanent, whether there were physical and demographic limits to suburbanization, whether the massive malls (none of which had been built in East Tennessee) would become the suburbanites' "new downtowns." In sum, these downtown entrepreneurs were intelligent men and women, but, obscured by their own hopes and fears, their vision was hardly prophetic. And even if they had possessed the hindsight we now possess, their financial resources were so modest that it is doubtful that they could have implemented bolder plans. As will be seen later, local banks were hardly more imaginative. In short, it would be appallingly unjust to pillory downtown merchants without fully understanding both their plight and their resources.

In truth, if anything, downtown retailers merely reflected a general conservatism and fearfulness that seems to have permeated nearly the entire local populace, including its political leaders. The 1956 "debate" between Cas Walker and J.S. Cooper, a former political protégé of Walker and city councilman in 1954–55 and 1956–57, illustrates the level to which the city's politics had sunk. This series of verbal duels ended in a fistfight that made national and even international headlines, though more as a spectacle than as a significant event. Initially the public argument erupted over the two men's respective tax assessments. Cooper claimed that Walker had used his markets' radio and newspaper ads to criticize Cooper. Since Cooper could not retaliate in kind, he used the city council meeting as a forum in which to defend himself. According to the *News-Sentinel* reporter, when Walker interrupted him, Cooper shouted, "Shut up until I finish."

"You make me," retorted Walker.

"Somebody *will* make you some day," said Cooper.

Walker's rejoinder was, "I've never run from anyone yet, and I won't run from you."

Having descended to the level of childish abuse, the two combatants

Fistfight at city council meeting, Cas Walker (left) vs. Jim Cooper, March 1956

KNOXVILLE *Journal*

seemed content to stay there while all of Knoxville looked on. Cooper accused Walker of getting preferred tax assessments; Walker countered that Cooper, his former political protégé, had had a chain link fence put up on his property at city expense ("I did everything I could to get Cooper elected, and he traded me off for a chain link fence"). At this point Cooper resorted to what was, for the 1950s, the ultimate insult, asserting that Walker "was using his usual Hitler and Stalin tactics, telling half-truths, no truths at all, and just plain lies."[50]

A month later the two clashed again, this time over the peanut and pop-corn concessions at Chilhowee Park. Walker and Cooper exchanged words, and Walker allegedly told Cooper, "You're going to keep on till I have to take you out and whip you."

Cooper replied, stooping inelegantly to the nadir of local political insult, "I'll meet you anywhere, you smart rat!"

Walker's rejoinder is unrecorded, but it was enough to make Cooper rush the grocer-councilman, daring him to take a swing at him. "I couldn't disappoint him," Walker later remembered.[51]

This account of the uproar staged by Walker and Cooper (dubbed "Pop-corn Jim" Cooper by Walker) is not intended to imply either that there were no political figures in Knoxville who rose above high school locker-room behavior or that there were no issues of sufficient importance for politicians to discuss. As we have seen, Dance had more than his share of vision, and the personal decorum of such men as John T. O'Connor, who was a former mayor, a city councilman, and a welfare director, and Max Friedman, who was a board member of the National Conference of Christians and Jews, a KHL member, and a city councilman, clearly puts Knoxville politics in a better light. And unquestionably there *were* crucial issues that urgently needed to be addressed. Yet in Knoxville good civic leaders never seemed to come to grips with crucial issues, and the city seemed regularly to be side-tracked by antics like the Walker-Cooper joust. Many of the voters who earlier might have demanded action had moved beyond the city limits into the more affluent suburbs. With a few exceptions, the UT and TVA newcom-ers tended to stay well behind the walls of their respective citadels. Those voters who remained in the city tended to reinforce the area's traditional conservatism. Against this potent combination, the forces of change fared poorly.

In many respects the issue of city-county consolidation was a good test of government and public reaction to change, especially in the period under analysis here. In the mid-1950s Tennessee's Ninetieth General Assembly

[50]*News-Sentinel*, Mar. 7, 1956: "Cooper-Walker throw fists at Council Meeting."
[51]*News-Sentinel*, Apr. 3, 1956; Walker interview, Feb. 21, 1977.

authorized consolidation of county and city governmental functions in areas where the population had grown to 200,000. It was "a way to enable local governments to deal with burgeoning suburban growth." The act authorized an election for consolidation by city and county voters separately, after a metro charter was recommended to and filed with the county election commission. In 1957 a charter commission was appointed in Knoxville. After nineteen months of study, both major newspapers and most officials of Knoxville and Knox County governments supported the consolidation of the two governments. But opposition, led by county employees, city teachers, and Cas Walker, continued to mount.[52]

The consolidation vote, coming at the end of a decade of significant change, was crucial. Its proponents saw its passage as a step into a sort of urban maturity and an escape from the city's turbulent industrial adolescence. That latter heritage, which many increasingly viewed as linked to a political immaturity, was still vociferously represented by Cas Walker. Ex-Mayor Walker, who served on all five city councils in the 1950s, seemed an elemental force in politics; blunt, acerbic, tough, and eternal, he could probably deliver 20,000 votes on any issue on a given day. Walker remained a strong fiscal conservative. When Mayor James Elmore, pleased by a low budget deficit at the beginning of the decade, called for reduced expenditures and the maintenance of government at the same tax rates, Walker supported him strongly against the objections of ex-mayor and "elder statesman" John T. O'Connor, who claimed, "I'm at a loss to understand why the biggest business of the city, the business of government, continues year after year on the same tax rate in the face of rising costs and increasing demand for services." Cas Walker's only response to this was to claim that the tax rate was already too high. Walker's fiscal conservatism was probably not as offensive to many of the city's real and self-appointed elite members as was his political style, which could be savage but was often simply a vulgar embarrassment to those who wanted desperately to transcend Knoxville's Appalachian image, a problem that had become acute since Walker's national exposure in 1956.[53]

Much was at stake, then, in the charter debate. As Gray and Adams have noted,

> On January 9, 1959, the charter commission filed its report with the Knox County Election Commission, which set April 9, 1959, as the

[52]Deaderick, ed., *Heart of the Valley*, 123.

[53]*News-Sentinel*, Jan. 5, 1950. Throughout most of the 1950s, despite increasing city budgets, the tax rate remained low. The *News-Sentinel* noted that in 1957 the rate "was still $2.64 per $100 of assessed valuation" despite the second highest budget in city history (the highest was 1956). *News-Sentinel*, Mar. 1, 1957.

date for the referendum on the proposed metropolitan government charter. The charter would vest legislative authority in a metropolitan council of ten members elected for four-year terms; the executive power would be vested in a metropolitan chairman elected at large for a four-year term. The total area of Knox County would receive such governmental services as police, courts, jails, health, welfare, hospitals, streets, airport, auditorium, public housing, parks and recreation, library, planning, urban renewal, building codes and ordinances, utilities, public transit, refuse disposal, and general regulation. An urban services district would be created which would receive, in addition to the services already named, fire protection, public water supply, sanitary sewers, storm sewers, street lighting, street cleaning, refuse collection, and a higher level of police protection. Additional taxes would be levied on the urban services district in order to fund the higher level of services needed for its denser population.[54]

Lee Greene, once executive secretary of the drafting commission of the charter and head of UT's political science department, told a group of one hundred PTA leaders from outside the city that approval of the charter would help attract industry: "I'm having to fight off requests for copies of the charter proposal now." Greene argued that in the event of consolidation, the county would be represented on the metropolitan commission, which would have the power to annex, whereas under current law the Knoxville city council could annex by simple vote, and the county inhabitants would not be represented. Greene also countered rumors about the exorbitant cost of installing sewers in fringe areas by pointing out that it had been a "frightful mistake to allow subdivisions to be built outside the city without sewer lines and six-inch water pipes."[55]

The Knoxville League of Women Voters, the Technical Society of Knoxville, and the American Society for Public Administration planned public study talks. The talks were later supported by the Chamber of Commerce, the Jaycees, the Knox County Council of Community Clubs, the Knoxville Ministerial Association, and the local AFL-CIO. In a panel debate over consolidation, some typical arguments for and against the proposal emerged. Dr. Edward Overman of UT's political science department argued that consolidation would attract business because it was "progressive." George Dempster, generally acknowledged to have a political base among the city teachers, argued against consolidation because he feared that the city teachers' pension fund would be diluted by "taking in the teachers from the county's hills and valleys." Dempster also disputed Overman's claim that

[54] Deaderick, ed., *Heart of the Valley*, 127.
[55] *News-Sentinel*, Jan. 14, 1959: "All eyes on Metro vote, Greene says."

new industries would come to Knoxville because of consolidation and allegedly added, "I don't think Knoxville should be a guinea pig for this kind of thing."[56]

For his part, Cas Walker apparently felt even more strongly about city-county consolidation. Darkly alleging that metropolitan government was communist-inspired, Walker distributed as "documentation" an article by Jo Hindman in the *American Mercury* entitled "Terrible 1313." Some businesspeople later recalled that "these allegations were sufficient to dampen the expected business enthusiasm." One of them, a former Knox County Republican party chairman, said, "We had expected that the civic groups, the Chamber of Commerce, civic clubs and groups like that would lead the fight for metro. They didn't because it was too controversial. Cas Walker was using his television programs and newspaper ads to claim that metro was Communistic. He was distributing these pamphlets about 1313."[57]

In the public study talks held at UT at the end of February, the City Teachers League expressed fears that their "sound" pension fund would be lost. Countering boldly if not diplomatically, Lee Greene argued that the pension fund was in fact already unsound. Several references were made to the circulation of "Terrible 1313" and to its allegation that metro government was part of an international movement to destroy democracy. One of the main speakers for consolidation, Victor Hobday of the university's Municipal Technical Advisory Service, said of this: "Some people would have you believe metropolitan government is un-American, even connected to Moscow. It is a sad commentary on the intelligence of this community." Hobday later referred to a statement allegedly made by Cas Walker: "This metropolitan chairman would have more power than Adolph Hitler."[58]

Attorney Harley Fowler, a member of the charter commission, believed that in spite of "cheap power and natural resources and the presence of UT and Oak Ridge, new industries generally shunned the area because of its byzantine politics." Moreover, Fowler pointed out that utility districts outside the city that had the sole right to supply water simply could not supply enough to prospective industries. The loss of industrial development, he

[56]Ibid., Jan. 29, 1959, and Feb. 23, 1959: "Panelists praise, assail metro."

[57]Baker, "Politics of Innovation," 70. Walker was notorious in his dislike of outside interests, real or imagined. As a member of the city council, Walker apparently tried to gag debate on a city school budget and was reportedly told by an Oak Ridge engineer, A.P. Fraas, that "it was a disgrace to let schools suffer to cut two cents off your taxes." Walker allegedly offered to throw Fraas off the platform, and finding out that Fraas had come to the area from Cleveland, Ohio, "Mr. Walker then said something about one of these smart alecks come down here to try to tell us how to run our affairs." *News-Sentinel*, Feb. 28, 1959: "School budget gag vote sets off row at council."

[58]*News-Sentinel*, Mar. 1, 1959.

further stated, had caused deteriorating real estate values downtown and concomitantly higher tax burdens on county residents. It was time, said Fowler, "to wipe the slate clean."[59]

As the April 9 consolidation vote neared, political rhetoric became even more turbulent. One newspaper article noted "officeholders put bite on workers to fight metro" and asserted that county employees were being "billed" ten dollars each: "Democratic office-holders are tapping their favorite source of campaign revenue—their low-salaried employees—to fight consolidation of city and county governments. . . ." Another article headed "anti-metro notes bring P.O. warning" disclosed that mailboxes had been stuffed with bogus promissory notes. Two check-sized sheets, with legal language copied from real promissory notes," referred to a $36-million city debt and $300 sewer-extension fees "which I (or my kids) promise to New York bankers and/or metro dictator." A *News-Sentinel* editorial, "City Teachers' Low Tactics Terrify Us," described "tension and fear among certain government employees." Referring to "scurrilous and wholly untrue allegations" of the City Teachers League, the editorial concluded that "city teachers are caught in the same company with unscrupulous politicians, race-baiters, and hate-mongers." This last referred to "convicted race-baiter and hate-monger" John Kasper, whose "hate sheet" in the week before the election urged Knoxville's citizens to vote against metro government. Cas Walker accused consolidation supporters of having issued the hate sheet under Kasper's name to discredit anti-metro forces, calling the incident the "lowest, dirtiest political trick I've ever seen." On the day before the vote, the *News-Sentinel* noted that Walker had refused to retract his charge that consolidation supporters had issued the sheet under Kasper's name, despite Kasper's acknowledgment that he himself had written it and left it with a local White Citizens' Council to distribute.[60]

As anticipated, consolidation was doomed. County voters refused to be saddled with what they saw as the albatross of a sinking city, and large blocs of city voters rejected this method of dealing with suburbanization and other problems. As if cowed by rhetoric alone, many business leaders preferred to sit out the referendum rather than risk being tarred with the brush of political radicalism. Again, conservatism and fear carried the day. The city retained archaic boundaries, within which demographic, transportation, and economic problems threatened to strangle the once-proud industrial center. While audiences might chuckle knowingly at Paul Soper's satire, the city limped toward the postindustrial age, an age that it might be prohibited from entering.

[59]Ibid., Apr. 4, 1959.
[60]Ibid., Apr. 6, 1959; Apr. 7, 1959; and Apr. 8, 1959.

URBAN FRUSTRATION AND CIVIL RIGHTS

As the nation's cities were faced with the serious problems of suburbanization, automobility, and downtown decay, urban residents vented their frustration and rage on both sides of the civil rights demonstrations of the 1950s. As upwardly mobile whites moved to the suburbs, urban populations more and more were composed of poor whites, blacks, and the elderly of both races. With job opportunities declining relative to population, with housing stock deteriorating daily, with television constantly beaming out messages of abundance and good times, and with national attention since the 1954 Supreme Court decision increasingly focused on the denial of civil rights to blacks, it was almost natural that blacks and sympathetic whites would begin to press for a more just society. Although, as we have seen, the real problems were demographic and economic, national attention tended to center on the racial integration of public facilities and private enterprises serving the public (movie theaters, restaurants, lunch counters).

Up to 1960 Knoxville had been comparatively free of racial tension. Though there had been trouble in nearby Clinton in the 1950s, Knoxville had remained the city that had traditionally prided itself on good race relations and steady if slow progress in black education, housing, and jobs. In some ways, of course, that progress had been entirely illusory, a fact indirectly attested to by the rather steady black out-migration that had been going on since the 1930s. For blacks who remained in Knoxville, job opportunities, housing stock, and access to quality public education had hardly advanced in the past forty years.

The failure to open the doors to economic mobility, combined with the pitifully slow progress in achieving their civil rights, caused many younger blacks, principally students at Knoxville College, to question the gradualist approach of black community leaders. In the spring of 1960, in a stormy meeting at Knoxville College, black students rejected the pleas of their elders, who argued that demonstrations would destroy all that they and white business leaders had been working steadily to achieve. Instead, as in other cities, the students decided to force the racial integration of restaurants and lunch counters through the sit-in technique. Nervously Knoxville braced for trouble.

On the whole, the demonstrations were orderly, and the massive violence many feared failed to materialize. Some ugly incidents did occur, but one observer believed that most of them had been fomented by whites from outside the city. Generally police were fair, if not overly sympathetic to the demonstrators' goals. However, so many shoppers avoided downtown that eventually fifty-five local merchants, led by Mayor John Duncan, agreed to integrate lunch counters, restaurants, hotels, motels, and theaters as quickly as possible. By 1967 the Urban League said that Knoxville had the "appearance of an open city."[61]

Yet while many blacks understandably took pride in their ability to force the white community to open its doors to them, Knoxville's sit-in demonstrations failed to alter the basic economic and social fabric of the city. Few whites, even among supposedly liberal UT faculty and TVA employees, actively supported the demonstrators. Moreover, the gains, while important symbolically, were really quite modest in terms of the real problems of Knoxville's black community.[62]

Indeed, in the troubled Knoxville of the 1950s, the real problems touched nearly everyone—white as well as black, old resident as well as recent arrival, rich as well as poor. Caught in the lag of the postindustrial age, the city seemed to lack the financial resources, the leadership, the unity, or the will to confront the trends and dilemmas of the 1950s. As some concerned citizens began to talk of Knoxville's need to "catch up" with the times, Paul Soper's *Once Upon a Town* gave them an outlet, an opportunity to laugh at themselves and their agonies and frustrations.

---

[61]J. Harvey Kerns, *Social and Economic Conditions in Knoxville, Tennessee, As They Affect the Negro* (Atlanta, 1967), 50. This was prepared for the National Urban League.

[62]Merrill Proudfoot, *Diary of a Sit-In* (New Haven, 1962), 142. Some TVA people did participate. See ibid., 61.

LONG-TIME OBSERVERS of Knoxville's business and political scenes sensed that Kyle Testerman was a different breed. Less inhibited by local traditions, mores, and fears, Testerman was an unashamed maverick, a man of boundless energy, great ambition, and even greater dreams. When he became mayor in 1971, after a bitter election campaign against incumbent Leonard Rogers, there was the general feeling that things would be different.

Those differences can be accounted for less by Testerman's background than by his personality and by the business and political faction he represented. Born in 1934 in Knoxville (his father had moved to Knoxville from Rogersville to practice law and get into the development business), Testerman graduated from UT Law School in 1958 and followed his father's footsteps into the development business, initially with the Tennessee Title Company. His interest in development and his political ambition prompted him to seek (unsuccessfully) the position of register of deeds, then to secure a spot on the MPC (1968–1972), and finally to win a seat on the city council (1970–1971). That seat gave Testerman the public exposure to launch his campaign for mayor.

This step-by-step advancement in both business and politics was hardly unique among Knoxville's political leaders. Where Testerman differed from others was his personality and the sources of his political support. Essentially an impatient man, he yearned to put an end to booster talk and planning, and get down to work. "I'd seen so much money spent on plans," Testerman said. "Why, you could have *rebuilt* Knoxville with the money they'd spent on plans." Instead, he attacked Knoxville's problems on all fronts, rewarding those who shared his vision and publicly mocking those more conservative or timid. "My goal was to drag Knoxville kicking and screaming into the twentieth century," he stated, even his language bristling with verbs of force and action. To Testerman, no obstacle was too large, no opponent too powerful, no vision too grand. In one sense, he was the modern version of Henry Grady and the New South boosters.

Testerman's political support came from a comparatively new force in Knoxville's economic and political life, a bloc of business-developers who had been involved in building the new western suburbs and new office complexes (like Testerman's ambitious development of the Northshore office buildings at the corner of Paper Mill Road and Northshore Drive), and who had begun to see the old downtown as a fruitful area for their attentions. More recently risen to wealth than the leaders of the Chamber of Commerce, this business-developer bloc was composed of young mavericks on the business and political scene. "We were suspect in the more staid business community, principally because we were too impatient to wait for things to happen by themselves."[1] These men had little sympathy for older ideas and methods and little patience with the slow wheels of Knoxville's traditional government. They saw their tasks as nothing less than bold planning for area growth and a massive renovation of downtown. More cosmopolitan than members of the business-progressive bloc that was alternately their ally and rival, these men longed for rapid change in a region notably resistant to either rapidity or change.[2]

Yet, by the early 1980s it still was not clear whether the business-developer bloc and their ideological and political allies had been able to turn Knoxville in new directions, for all their energy, ambition, and newly acquired power. Forces opposing change were still extremely powerful, joining the traditional Appalachian and old elite conservatism with newer strains that opposed the most blatant forms of boosterism and "progress for its own sake" mentality. In part victims of their own excesses and style, the business-developers had yet to prove that they could change a city so resistant to change. For Knoxville, then, like the New South of Henry Grady's generation, the visions of the Appalachian city's golden age remained just over the next horizon.

THE AMERICAN CITY IN THE POSTINDUSTRIAL AGE

In general, the 1960s and 1970s were troubled times for America's cities. Those dependent on heavy durable-goods manufacturing faced economic difficulties in almost direct proportion to the extent of the ill health of their particular industries. Blacks, Puerto Ricans, and southern whites fleeing rural poverty continued to add to these troubled cities' economic and social strains. Moreover, as these people poured into the cities in search of opportunities, lower-middle-class and middle-class whites fled in more than equal numbers, in some cases causing absolute declines in urban populations (the most dramatic being that of St. Louis, which suffered a 27-percent drop in population during the 1970s, most of those who fled being lower-middle-class and middle-class whites). Strange neighbors and their even stranger ways, disturbingly rising crime rates, and increasing tax burdens drove

[1]Interview with Kyle Testerman, Jan. 22, 1981.
[2]Ibid.

whites out of cities they felt were no longer theirs. Their departures meant that an important source of revenue for cities was drying up. With those who fled went many of the retail merchants, who followed neighbors and dollars into burgeoning suburban shopping malls. They left behind them cities increasingly populated by the black, the poor, the aged—those whom modernization had left behind.

Some cities were able to control such economic and population erosions. Most did so by attracting "new line" industries (electronics, fabricated metals, synthetics, and chemicals) to their rims and beltways; these industries drew high-salaried employees who gave boosts both to construction trades and retail establishments. In turn, those newcomers created a demand for goods, services, educational institutions, and cultural attractions that further stimulated those fortunate cities. Of course, in fact "fortune" had little to do with the successes of these cities, for those who had been able to lure "new line" industries (thereby becoming successful in the "postindustrial" age while "old line" industries declined) had done so through aggressive sales campaigns, favorable land acquisition policies, good interstate highway connections, and friendly political leaders. From the 1960s on, those cities became the models for all of urban America.

As noted in chapter 3, Knoxville by the early 1960s was a city in trouble. The city's industrial base (durable-goods manufacturing, with a heavy emphasis on textiles and apparel) had experienced mounting difficulties, so much so that between 1948 and 1960 approximately 4,200 manufacturing jobs had evaporated. Jobs in construction also had declined, and the service sector, which on the national level had taken up much of the decade's employment slack, in Knoxville grew only slowly. The service industries' failure to fill the city's employment vacuum was due to the area's exceedingly low wage scale. With 46 percent of Knoxville's and Knox County's industrial employees earning under $5,000 per year and with apparel workers averaging $3,100 per year, it would be surprising if the service sector had been healthy. At those wages, men and women simply lacked the discretionary income to spend for services. Add to that a SMSA unemployment rate of 7.7 percent in 1961, and one has the disturbing picture of a city still in the grips of a real economic dilemma. While these problems were hardly new to Knoxville, since they were part of a pattern that went back at least fifty years, by the early 1960s they had become so serious that they threatened Knoxville's very existence.[3]

Especially crucial were forces that seemed to make the attraction of "new line" industries and their many benefits a virtual impossibility. As shown

[3] Hammer and Associates, "The Economy of Metropolitan Knoxville" (study proposed for the Metropolitan Planning Commission, 1962), 16–17, 26–27, 30–31, 64–68; RERC, *Trends, Conditions, and Forecasts of Knoxville's Economy*, 40–42, 53.

above, American cities which had been successful in doing so had aggressively sought out and lured such industries, had established favorable terms (including industrial parks) for land acquisition, had been linked into the developing interstate highway system (which fitted "new line" needs better than did the declining railroads), had maintained a politically friendly climate for development, and had avoided social tensions and racial problems that tended to scare newcomers away. But in Knoxville all of these factors appeared to be obstacles to the city's changing direction in the postindustrial age.

To begin with, much of the city's traditional business elite (which had shown tendencies toward economic, social, and political conservatism since the turn of the century) seems to have preferred Knoxville as it was. This group was unfriendly to new enterprises that might either compete for the skilled labor pool or be more receptive to unionization. A proposed bond referendum that would have raised money to purchase a building for a sizable business interested in locating in the city was opposed by the Chamber of Commerce and a majority of Knoxville's business people on the grounds that public money should not be used to assist private enterprises. In fact, as then-Mayor John Duncan recalled, "A man sat in that very chair and said it was good to have an unemployment rate of 6 or 7 percent because it made people work harder."[4]

By the early 1960s a good portion of the city's old elite families derived much of their income from the ownership of downtown real estate. To them, plans to rejuvenate the center city meant that property values would rise, hiking property taxes. Hence, this group often sided with men like Cas Walker (whom they personally ridiculed and abhorred), whose constituency often opposed change for other reasons. Downtown merchants seemed interested in little but schemes to improve downtown retail trade, and therefore they did not participate in the 1959 metropolitan government referendum and later opposed the industrial bond referendum.[5] The closely knit and elite family-controlled banking houses displayed a marked reluctance to take risks with new people or business ventures. Stunned by the financial reverses of the Great Depression, they developed an even more cautious mind-set that made them suspicious of any but the safest investments or loans.[6]

The bolder business-developer bloc that emerged in the mid-1960s (whose titular head was Kyle Testerman) openly ridiculed local bankers for their timidity. "When you have an executive of a major local bank earning

[4]Baker, "Politics of Innovation," 72.
[5]Ibid., 69.
[6]White, "Banking Developments," in Deaderick, ed., *Heart of the Valley*, 379–89.

around $16,000 a year, it's hard for him to *conceive* of someone wanting to borrow a couple of million dollars for a new business venture," Testerman later remarked. Testerman's opinion of local bankers as people who lacked vision and imagination dated back to his initial attempts to seek local financing for his ambitious Northshore office buildings: "The whole bank board sat around and wrung their hands when I presented my idea. Finally one of them said, 'Well, Mr. Testerman, what will happen if you fail?' I told them, 'Well, then you'll have the biggest damn bank building in West Knoxville.' [Laughs] That just scared the hell out of them." Knoxville's bankers, like the traditional elite to which they belonged, seem to have feared change, whether it came from "outsiders" (potential "new-line" industries) or from Knoxvillians like Testerman who challenged both their views and their power.[7]

Yet the city's elite merely mirrored the general conservatism of the community, a resistance to change that had many sources. Tax increases were consistently rejected, even in the face of pressing needs to maintain services and schools, to attract more visitors (who in 1961 accounted for only 9 percent of all Knoxville's retail business) by building a civic coliseum-auditorium, and to extend services (the most pressing of which was sewers) to recently annexed areas. In 1966 those who supported a scheme to raise the city's tax ceiling were routed by the voters, 34,000 to 6,000, with those areas most in need of increased services (especially Beaumont) most firmly against the increases. Most prominent among the opponents of increased taxes, of course, was Cas Walker, once more a rallying point for the enemies of change. His popularity apparently undiminished by two brawls he had engaged in during city council meetings in the 1950s, Walker opposed virtually every scheme for meeting the city's dilemmas. In addition to his 1959 defeat of the proposal for metropolitan government and his blocking in the 1960s of the construction of a shoppers' mall in an area where the old Market House had been located, Walker also: opposed annexation on the grounds that it would increase taxes; tried to halt purchase of downtown property for a new public library; fought against both the consolidation of the health department (which threatened his patronage power) and flouridation of the city's water; halted attempts to build a civic coliseum; and aroused the people against the construction of a new city-county government building. Through all of this, Walker spoke for those, white and black, rich and poor, who feared that change would be accomplished only at terrible financial and psychological costs. Truly, though Walker was an embarrassment to some, for many (even for some of those who would not admit him to their

[7]Interview with Testerman, Jan. 22, 1981.

fashionable circles) he was the most consistent defender of Knoxville as they wanted it to remain.[8]

It would be unfair, however, to place total blame for Knoxville's failure to attract "new line" industries in the 1950s and early 1960s on the city's old elite or its conservative citizenry. Forces often beyond the control of Knoxvillians also counted for some of the city's inability to break its apparent paralysis. For one thing, cities that had successfully attracted "new line" industries had established good interstate highway connections. But Knoxville had been unable to do so. The difficulties of building highways in the hilly region must be considered one important factor, but most observers also believed that the East Tennessee city, which voted Republican constantly, had been denied new highways by the Democratic governors and the Democratic-controlled state legislature. The story may be apocryphal, but it was often said in Knoxville that the Democratic governor, when approached by Knoxvillians seeking interstate connections, replied, "When you people learn to vote right, you'll get your roads." Hence intrastate political party rivalries apparently cut Knoxville off from the life-giving interstate highway system.

Moreover, the city lacked the skilled labor pool necessary for "new line" industries. Those skilled workers who did exist in Knoxville had been snapped up by ALCOA and Oak Ridge, neither of which was expanding in the 1950s. And as jobs dried up, both skilled and unskilled workers began to abandon the city, leaving behind the young (those under fourteen increased from 25.1 percent of the population to 27.2 percent between 1950 and 1960), the old (sixty-five and over increased from 6.6 percent to 9.5 percent), and those increasingly immobilized by poverty.[9]

Southern cities that hoped to attract "new line" industries had to prove they were free from racial friction. But again Knoxville failed to meet this important criterion. By 1960 the city's black population for the most part was employed in domestic service (56 percent of the black working males and 73 percent of black working females) and unskilled jobs. Wages were almost uniformly low, the black family's median income in 1960 being only $2,237. Over half of Knoxville's blacks lived in slum conditions, one slum (Mountain View) so bad that in 1960 it was rated 20,875th of 20,915 urban census tracts in the entire nation in terms of housing stock. Illegitimacy, crime, and poor health were all high.[10]

Black leadership long had chosen to work with the white elite for long-

[8]*News-Sentinel*, Oct. 23, 1960; *Journal*, Dec. 29, 1960; May 4, 1968; interview with Lee S. Greene, Feb. 15, 1977; Jo Hindman, "Terrible 1313," *American Mercury* 84 (Jan. 1959): 5–15; Baker, "Politics of Innovation," 70, 111, 220.

[9]*U.S. Census*, 1950 and 1960.

[10]Kerns, *Social and Economic Conditions in Knoxville*, 2, 52.

range improvement of conditions rather than to challenge the elite and the city's informal but rigid codes of racial segregation. But, as shown above, younger blacks (principally students at the predominantly black Knoxville College) were determined to challenge those barriers directly in the 1960 lunch counter sit-in demonstrations. They had little support among or help from white Knoxvillians: UT faculty members who supported the demonstrations were in the distinct minority; UT students were conspicuous by their absence; jeweler-councilman Max Friedman was the only white public official who openly supported the demonstrations; TVA employees, largely "outsiders" sympathetic to the sit-ins, were requested by TVA "for the sake of good public relations not to participate in any further demonstrations." Finally, Mayor John Duncan, a politically ambitious lawyer who was influential with the business community, persuaded Knoxville businesses to accept racial integration. Duncan seems to have understood in 1960 what a majority of white southerners did not: that any city tarred with the brush of racial strife would be years trying to erase an image that was obviously "bad for business." But while the demonstrations served the purpose of beginning to roll back the tides of racial segregation, they also made the city appear more racially troubled than in fact it probably was. Any hint of racial friction would act to scare away prospective new businesses.[11]

Finally, cities hoping to attract "new line" industries needed to demonstrate a political climate that was both stable and friendly to innovation and newcomers. Again, Knoxville could not do this in the 1950s or early 1960s. Viciously personal, often corrupt, and almost universally masters of a political style that Louis Brownlow earlier had called "East Tennessee screamology," Knoxville's political chieftans had waged brutal warfare almost solely to protect their modest baronies or to extend their influence. That the stakes appear to have been small mattered little; that local politics was so unstable that it might have frightened away potential new businesses and investors mattered not at all. Dempster had vision (especially concerning public education) but was willing to wink at the questionable dealings of others to achieve his goals. Walker himself was honest, but he spoke for a populace fearful of change and engaged in the most blatant forms of influence-peddling and cronyism. Guy Smith of the Knoxville *Journal* was a newspaperman in the best and worst sense of the word: independent, articulate, and willing to call dishonesty by its true name, he preferred instead to stoke up petty controversy and use the *Journal* to befriend his allies and castigate his enemies. When Dempster was in power, so the stories go, he used to delight in catching Smith's car double-parked (a habit of Smith's) so he could have the police tow it away. For his part, Friedman

[11] An excellent book on Knoxville's experience is Proudfoot, *Diary of a Sit-In*. On Max Friedman see Baker, "Politics of Innovation," 114.

cried for honesty and a businesslike approach to government, principles that had governed this remarkable man's business and life, but his integrity, honesty, and liberalism on social issues caused him to be regarded by other politicos as some species of village idiot. His secure place on city council, where he invariably voted in the minority, was an embarrassing reminder to Knoxvillians of what their local politics ought to have been—and was not.[12]

Several political observers believe that the city's unstable political situation was the principal discouragement to new business. "The savage infighting between men like Cas Walker and George Dempster often turned City Council meetings into three-ring circuses," one recalls. One councilman was rumored to have been connected with the bootleg liquor traffic, while another had been suspended from the certified public accountants' association for "failure to meet minimal professional standards in conducting the post-audit of the county's books."[13] Probably equally worrisome to potential new businesses was the high turnover of mayors and councilmen, which gave the distinct impression that the city was politically unstable. Clearly, Knoxville's political climate in the years from the end of World War II to the early 1960s was another factor that prevented the city from moving in new directions in the postindustrial age.

Hence, whether because of a conservative elite who preferred things as they were, of forces over which the city had comparatively little control, or of an apparently unstable political situation (or a combination of all of these), Knoxville in the 1950s and early 1960s was unable to attract "new line" industries, which were the key to success of postwar American cities. In 1961 only 12 people in the city were working for establishments that had begun in that year; 1962 showed only a minor increase, to 87 workers in new industries. Not surprisingly, with employment opportunities either static or in decline in nearly every sector, the city's population was failing to keep pace with natural increase, though that fact was obscured by massive 1962 annexations of West Hills, Bearden, Norwood, Gresham, and Fountain City. The city was in trouble.[14]

To be sure, few of these problems were unique to Knoxville; on the contrary, they were dilemmas facing nearly every American city at the beginning of the 1960s. What made Knoxville distinctive was its citizens' apparent failure of will. Its politicians were locked in savage but essentially meaningless battles; its bankers were cautious and timid to a fault; its working-age population was fleeing the city to the county or beyond; it was excessively defensive about its image, as if it felt John Gunther would

[12]On Dempster-Smith rivalry: interview with George Fritts (retired realtor and keen observer of Knoxville politics), Apr. 8. 1977.

[13]Ibid.; interview with Leonard Rogers, Jan. 17, 1981; Baker, "Politics of Innovation," 319–20.

[14]Hammer, "The Economy of Metropolitan Knoxville," 95–100, 122.

return. Knoxville entered the 1960s poorly equipped to confront its problems, problems faced by most American cities in the postindustrial age.

THE SEARCH FOR THE NEW CITY

Despite the city's problems, those who wrote epitaphs for Knoxville wrote prematurely. Beginning in the mid-1960s, a fortuitous combination of national trends, new political configurations, and good luck acted to arrest the decline, turn it around, and set the city on a new course. To be sure, serious problems persisted, and some people felt that the new directions were only short-term flurries rather than long-term trends. But by the mid-1970s few could deny that Knoxville was a vastly changed city from the one it had been but a decade before.

One could hardly have missed the changes. From 1965 through 1968, new industries located in the city and county, adding approximately 1,500 new jobs and roughly $7.5 million in capital investment. During the same period, over a hundred existing industries expanded their operations, adding around 6,300 jobs and over $41 million in capital investment. Significantly, a number of these new jobs (especially those at the upper echelons) were taken by newcomers, many of whom (7 percent of the metro work force by 1965) were scientific and technological employees and formed the nucleus of a new professional-managerial class. A high proportion settled in the rapidly expanding bedroom communities west of the center city, along the Kingston Pike–I-40 axis. By 1970 residential development had reached land previously in pasture over twenty miles from downtown, far beyond the city's expanding western limits. In terms of the area's per capita income, most of these newcomers were affluent men and women whose dollars stimulated construction and retail trade.[15]

Statistics for construction, retail trade, and services all showed dramatic increases. From 1964 through 1967, 1,559 building permits were granted in the city and 4,779 in the county, adding over $70 million to the area's economy. Employees in wholesale and retail trades had reached 30,800 by 1968, while employees in service industries increased 43.6 percent between 1960 and 1967. Even durable-goods manufacturing experienced some increase, though it was not significant and was mostly at the lower wage levels. Hence unemployment, which had been 7.7 percent in 1961, shrank to 2.8 percent in 1965 and was still under 4.0 percent in 1970.[16]

Physically the city was changing, too. The downtown area, once richly

[15]Stone and Webster Engineering Company, "Site Proposal for the New National Accelerator Laboratory" (a preliminary site survey for the City of Oak Ridge, June 1965), 106.
[16]Ibid., 124.

deserving of Gunther's barbs, underwent alterations. Facelifting the retail establishments on South Gay was mere cosmetology, but the Market Square Mall, the TVA twin towers, a new city-county government building, the Summit Hill project, the new United American Bank building, and plans for an east-west mall were not. Although an East-West Mall had been proposed as an alternative to the North-South Market Street Mall as early as 1961, it was more fully elaborated by Mayor Testerman's downtown task force as a pedestrian link between Gay and Locust streets behind the old post office (now the Customs House). This was clearly an attempt to "reanchor" Miller's and the older downtown businesses, and became a formal Knoxville Community Development Corporation (KCDC) proposal approved by city council in 1973.

Nor was it merely cosmetic to launch the efforts to clean up the riverfront area (previously known as "Shantytown") and undertake a major urban renewal project in Mountain View, a black neighborhood (on the site of the present Hyatt-Regency Hotel and the Safety Building) that President Lyndon Johnson described in 1964 as containing the worst poverty he had ever seen. In the 1960s, White's Fort, which had been dismantled and moved from its original site to private property on Woodlawn Pike in 1906, was restored on a bluff overlooking the changing city. While one could not boast in the mid-1970s that downtown Knoxville was a beautiful urban showplace, one could say that the city had overcome some of the worst features of its unattractiveness.[17]

Considerably more dramatic than Knoxville's economic or physical changes, however, was a new spirit evident in portions of the community. Less defensive, more able to admit the city's shortcomings, less willing to fall back on the "that's-a-good-idea-but-it-would-never-work-in- Knoxville" mentality, this new attitude was strengthened by the economic and physical progress that had been accomplished and made further changes possible, if not certain. John Gunther's earlier comments more often drew laughter than apoplectic anger. Indeed, by the mid-1970s some Knoxvillians thought in grand terms of hosting a world's fair. To be sure, this new spirit was considerably less than universal, but its appearance promised more changes—and conflicts—in the future.

Several factors were responsible for this change of direction. Most important were the impressive amounts of money that began to be pumped into the city by the mid-1960s. Government employment certainly was important. By 1967 there were over 16,000 federal and state employees working in the Knoxville SMSA, an increase of almost 65 percent over 1960. By 1970, 23 percent of the wage earners residing in the city worked for government at

[17]A.J. Gray, "Report to the Center City Task Force, May 1974" (MPC Library); Downtown Knoxville Association, *The Downtown Knoxville Story* (Knoxville, 1965).

some level. Moreover, government money—especially federal money—provided a tremendous boost to the city's economy. Between 1972 and 1976, Kyle Testerman's mayoral administration received approximately $84 million in revenue-sharing and federal grants. And that was only a fraction of the federal money pouring into the city in the form of food programs, loans, grants, salaries, pensions, and contracts. Indeed, according to one report, in 1979 the federal government spent roughly $1 billion in Knoxville.[18]

At the same time that Knoxville was receiving startling injections of federal money, other sources of revenue were expanding in an equally dramatic fashion. The University of Tennessee, which in the 1950s had been a modest campus on "the Hill" with about 5,000 students, by the mid-1970s had become a megaversity with just under 30,000 students. By 1967 it was estimated that the university annually added over $70 million to the community (exclusive of new construction), $36 million in payroll (up from an estimated $10 million in 1959) and the remainder spent in Knoxville by students as well as contracts to local jobbers for furniture, equipment, and materials. Construction contracts awarded by the expanding university (approximately $73 million in the decade from 1957 to 1967) further enriched the area. Though not all were delighted by the university's expansion (in the early 1960s the Yale Avenue neighborhood had not greeted warmly its westward expansion off the Hill south of Cumberland Avenue), clearly an important new economic force had been added to the community.[19]

The major annexation of 1962 brought the Fountain City area, as well as large portions of the rapidly expanding western regions, into Knoxville. Though providing services to these areas was initially expensive, the increased revenues gave city government a breathing space in the 1960s and early 1970s, before new financial demands began to close in. Equally important, according to former Mayor Leonard Rogers, was the fact that the people of the newly annexed areas came to see their collective future as being tied irrevocably to that of the city. As will be seen, those new voters significantly altered the political face of Knoxville.[20]

Initially, Fountain City dwellers had felt no kinship with Knoxville. A number of them had filed a lawsuit in 1960 (later dropped) to block Knoxville's annexation efforts. They feared that Knoxville would not provide crucial urban services (including some 400 miles of necessary water lines) but was only grasping for their tax dollars. But since 1959 the state legislature had permitted Tennessee cities to annex contiguous areas by city council action without holding a referendum. When the area ultimately was annexed in 1962, Fountain Citians held a parade and mock funeral service

[18]Interview with Testerman, Jan. 22, 1981; *News-Sentinel*, Nov. 16, 1980.
[19]RERC, *Trends, Conditions and Forecasts of Knoxville's Economy*, 187.
[20]Interview with Rogers, Jan. 17, 1981.

for their community, and one local businessman presented Knoxville mayor John Duncan with a sword of surrender. Yet, while many residents of Fountain City continued to resent the 1962 annexation (and corrected those who referred to them as "Knoxvillians"), the fact that they had not been involved in the city's past political warfare gave them a different perspective on city politics and on the city itself.[21]

Nor were these new voters the only groups who altered Knoxville's political configurations. In the early 1960s more aggressive elements within the elite-controlled Chamber of Commerce apparently were able to confront the city's political instability. For years they had been ashamed of the vicious, often corrupt, and highly flamboyant political scene but had become involved in the political fray only sporadically. By the mid-1960s those elements within the Chamber of Commerce had had enough. As an alternative to continued instability, they supported one of their own (Leonard Rogers) for mayor and captured control of the city council. Although they certainly would have denied it, these business leaders formed a Chamber of Commerce-oriented political faction that might best be called the "business-progressive" bloc. Possessing social and business connections that undoubtedly marked them as of the elite, they clearly were less conservative than their fathers and grandfathers had been. Max Friedman, who had served on the city council prior to the business-progressives' victory, told Rogers that the two years after Rogers's victory had been the "two happiest years of my life," since he was at last voting with the majority.[22]

At the same time that the business-progressive group was reentering the political arena, two other political blocs were forming that would have a major impact on the city in the 1970s. Potentially the most powerful was the large group of newcomers who came from outside the region to work for the "new line" industries attracted in the late 1960s. Though a large proportion lived outside the city, many others settled inside the post-1962 boundaries, especially along the western corridor in Sequoyah Hills, West Hills, and Bearden. Affluent, well-educated, more liberal than the general community in their social, economic, and political views, these men and women demanded what many of them had enjoyed elsewhere: efficient services, good educational facilities for their children, honest and visionary politics, and local beautification. They threw themselves into local PTAs, church groups, social and professional clubs, and civic groups such as the League of Women Voters. Recognizing that a "newcomer" would have little chance in any citywide election, they searched for those men and women bold and imaginative enough to earn their backing. They gave their votes to younger

---

[21]*News-Sentinel*, July 20, 1961; Feb. 11, 1962; Apr. 4, 1981.
[22]Interview with Rogers, Jan. 17, 1981.

candidates like Victor Ashe. Ashe was a native Knoxvillian from an impeccably elite family that had made a considerable fortune in the textile industry. He had graduated from Yale University and had shown some promise of ideological and political flexibility. Ashe saw his own future in the state legislature (though rumors of other political ambitions continue to surface) and, aided by the increasingly influential newcomers, in 1981 had never yet lost an election. Throughout the late 1960s newcomers continued to support local political figures like Ashe, for the school board, the city council, and other elected bodies.

The third and, in the short run, most potent new group to affect Knoxville politics in the mid-to-late 1960s was the business-developer bloc. More recently risen to wealth than those of the business-progressive bloc, this group was comparatively younger, more aggressive, and culturally less sophisticated than their business-progressive "betters." Not afraid to amass considerable debts to finance their construction and real estate development schemes, many (like their titular leader and spokesman Kyle Testerman) built impressive development empires on borrowed money. Frustrated by what they considered to have been the excessive timidity of the city's business elite and the resistance to change of its politicians, many drifted toward the political arena. Initially, they formed an alliance with the more established business-progressive bloc, a pact that ultimately was as shaky as it was unnatural.[23]

One important member of the business-developer bloc was banker Jake F. Butcher. Born in Dotson's Creek in Union County (approximately seven miles from Maynardville) in 1936, Butcher was the son of Cecil H. Butcher, Sr., who owned and operated a general store and in 1950 had organized the Union County Bank of Maynardville, a small operation that ultimately became the parent bank of the City and County (C&C) banking group. After attending the University of Tennessee, serving in the Marine Corps, spending a year at Hiwassee College, and then two more years at UT (he never graduated), Jake Butcher was ready to enter the business world. Although he founded the Bull Run Oil Company (an Amoco distributorship) and was engaged in commercial farming, his real interest was banking, the area in which he had served a long apprenticeship under his father (one longtime associate remembered that "he started in banking by sweeping the floors and then counting pennies and worked his way up"). In 1974, with capital borrowed from a number of regional banks, Butcher began purchasing stock in the Hamilton National Bank, at that time the city's largest banking institution with 39.2 percent of the city's total banking resources. In early 1975,

[23]Interview with Testerman, Jan. 22, 1981.

Victor Ashe

KNOXVILLE *News-Sentinel*

after a brief fight, Butcher won complete control of the bank and changed its name to United American.[24]

The Butcher victory represented more than just one man's personal triumph. As has been noted above, up to the time of the Butcher takeover Knoxville's bankers had been a closely knit, cautious fraternity, generally suspicious of new people (like the business-developer bloc) and radically new ideas. But Butcher's inclinations and thinking closely dovetailed with those of the business-developer bloc. Moreover, few at the time appreciated how fragile and vulnerable Butcher's banking empire was. His imagination, boldness, and willingness to take risks obliged other local banks to become more venturesome. Though Butcher's attention was often absorbed by two unsuccessful bids, in 1974 and 1978, to become state governor, his willingness to gamble on redevelopment and new industries made him—and the business-developer bloc—a major force in Knoxville's economic and political life. By 1982 the United American bank accounted for over half the business loans made in the city.

As these new forces in Knoxville's politics swelled in power, older political leaders and factions declined. Most notable was the political deterioration of Cas Walker, who had been a major factor to be reckoned with since the late 1930s. He did retain his old power bases among lower-middle-class and poor whites and blacks (especially in Wards Seven-N, Seven-S, Nine-N, Nine-S, Twelve, Thirteen, Fourteen, Sixteen, Nineteen, Twenty, Twenty-two, and Twenty-four-N. But in the 1960s these groups steadily declined as a proportion of the total voting population, as a continued exodus from the center city met the mushrooming of neighborhoods (especially Fountain City and West Knoxville) annexed to the city in 1962. To the legions of newcomers—upper-middle-class business and professional people from outside the region—Walker was a laughable but dangerous retrograde, a political neanderthal who (as Henry Adams once said of President Grant) should have been extinct for ages, or lived in a cave and worn skins. They failed to appreciate that Walker was more than a caricature of a regressive political style; that as much as anything else he was the representative of an Appalachian constituency; that he shared their distrust of change, of newcomers, of outsiders; and that he was the last political hope for citizens caught in the cogs of modernization. But now the savage warrior, who made no money personally from his years in local government but who had been generous with jobs and other favors to political friends, saw the political handwriting on the wall. In the eyes of the newcomers, he simply had to be eliminated.[25]

[24]Butcher biographical material collected from Public Relations Office of UAB and the *News-Sentinel* clippings file. On the struggle to acquire UAB see White, "Banking Developments," in Deaderick, ed., *Heart of the Valley*, 398–400.

[25]Walker's power base was identified through analysis of council election returns from 1941

In the November 1963 city council runoff among eight candidates, Walker placed a dismal eighth in three of the newly annexed wards, seventh in one, sixth in two, fifth in three, and nowhere higher than fourth. He did little better in 1967. "They was embarrassed to be seen votin' for an ole coal miner like me," Walker mused in 1977. Thus, though Cas Walker continued to win a place on the city council, with each election his margin of victory eroded and with it his power in that body. Finally, in 1971, faced with stern opposition and with the demographic cards stacked against him, he withdrew before the city council election, later maintaining that his wife had begged him not to run again. Thus ended an era in Knoxville politics that had lasted for nearly five decades. While Walker was far from silent, what influence he retained in the latter 1970s came from different and surprising new constituencies.[26]

Another factor responsible for the changing political climate and for the increased willingness of much of the city's population to look for new answers to old problems was the growing prosperity and political sophistication of some of the very areas that previously had generated potential Walker supporters. In the 1920s and 1940s most of Knoxville's in-migrants had come from the surrounding rural hinterland, seeking employment in the city's manufacturing industries. By the late 1960s, however, many of the children (or grandchildren) of these men and women had adjusted successfully to the demands of the urban environment and the industrial and postindustrial ages. Education, vocational training, decades of urban living, and the communications revolution had made them all aware of the values and expectations of middle-class urban society. In many cases two generations had been sufficient for these people to absorb the entire immense urban revolution.[27]

Studies of two Knoxville city wards attest to this generally successful adjustment by some in-migrants to urban life and demands. Wards Thirty-six (Gresham) and Forty (Norwood) in the northern part of the city are settled, middle-class areas that experienced considerable in-migration from the Appalachian hinterland in the waves of both the 1920s and the 1940s. A 1977 study showed that only 42.1 percent and 42.9 percent, respectively, of a sample of the wards' 1976 registered voters had been born in Knox County. Most adults in the sample were members of skilled labor groups, and an impressive proportion (64 percent) either owned their own homes or lived

---

through 1957. See *News-Sentinel*, Nov. 7, 1941; Nov. 5, 1943; Nov. 2, 1945; Dec. 4, 1946 (recall election); Nov. 7, 1947; Nov. 8, 1957.

[26]Interview with Cas Walker, Feb. 21, 1977; on strength see *Journal*, Nov. 8, 1963; Nov. 3, 1967.

[27]John D. Photiadis has found this pattern in his studies of Cleveland, Ohio. See his *West Virginians in Their Own State and in Cleveland, Ohio: Summary and Conclusions of a Comparative Social Study*, Appalachian Center Information Report no. 3 (West Virginia Univ., 1970).

with relatives who did so. Most interesting, out of twenty-one Knoxville city planning units in 1970, Gresham and Norwood ranked thirteenth and seventeenth, respectively, in cumulative severity of school dropouts, venereal disease, adult arrests, juvenile delinquency, and number of families receiving public assistance. Clearly, in these neighborhoods, the children and grandchildren of the in-migrants had adjusted successfully to the rigors of urban life. Better-paying jobs produced higher incomes (by 1977 Norwood's mean income was $15,496 as compared with the entire city's average of $11,190), bringing a measure of financial security and an opportunity to participate more fully in the consumer culture of the 1960s and 1970s. More to the point, economic mobility made these men and women more receptive to new ideas, more inclined to support political figures who possessed visions of a new Knoxville. More confident and less fearful than their in-migratory parents and/or grandparents had been, they hoped to ride the crest of the new wave, send their own children into the business and professional class (through the avenue of college educations), and adopt a lifestyle that their parents and/or grandparents both ridiculed and envied.[28]

Hence, several factors were responsible for Knoxville's reawakening in the 1960s: federal money; the mushrooming of the university; new political blocs of business-progressives, business-developers, and upper-middle-class newcomers; bolder banking practices; the political decline of Cas Walker; the economic and social mobility of the children and grandchildren of many Appalachian in-migrants. Although these forces did not always move in the same direction in a unified, harmonious fashion, and new directions were not universally endorsed or logically conceived, clearly these forces together tended to produce a climate more receptive to change than any other in Knoxville in the twentieth century.

ROGERS, TESTERMAN, AND THE POLITICS OF CHANGE

To those who, in the mid-1960s, sought to move the city into new paths, it appeared that the greatest stumbling block to progress was the local political situation. Since the demise of the city-manager form of government in the

---

[28] For statistics on birthplaces, occupations, lengths of residence in Knoxville, and home ownership, see Voter Registration Books, Knox County Election Commission. For correlation of these areas to social problems see Knoxville–Knox County Community Action Committee, *Poverty in Knoxville and Knox County* (Knoxville, 1973), 23. It is interesting to note that most areas housing Appalachian in-migrants, whether of lower- or middle-class character, have a strikingly low percentage of blacks. See ibid., 14. One disturbing aspect of the populations of Wards 36 and 40 is that the areas appear to be failing over the past decades to hold their young populations, another indication of the city's inability to absorb even its own skilled population. See Voter Registration Books, Knox County Election Commission.

1940s, political power in Knoxville had been so evenly balanced among personal factions that bold policies had been avoided and turnover in office had been high. Voters had been fickle, tending to cast their ballots for those who promised to keep taxes low, even at the risk of essential services. In referendum after referendum, most voters seem to have wanted to keep things as they were.

But by the mid-1960s those new forces in Knoxville (business-progressives, business-developers, and upper-middle-class newcomers) had had enough of the old ways. Each group was ready to test its strength in the political arena. Thus, when Mayor John Duncan won election to the U.S. House of Representatives in late 1964, the way was open for these groups to replace him with one of their own. The man selected for support was Leonard Rogers. Rogers had come to Knoxville from Shelby County in 1932 to attend UT on a 4-H Club scholarship. Majoring in agriculture and graduating in 1937 ("It took us a little longer to go through school during the Depression," Rogers remembers), he took a job with Security Mills, a large feed manufacturing concern. There he stayed for eighteen years, achieving the position of regional sales manager for East Tennessee. First coming to the attention of the business-progressive bloc in the mid-1950s when he became secretary-manager of the Tennessee Valley Fair, Rogers was elected president of the Chamber of Commerce in the late 1950s. When Councilman Ernest J. (Ernie) O'Connor died in office in 1964, the business-progressives persuaded Mayor Duncan to appoint Rogers to fill the vacancy on the city council. In the 1965 special election to fill Duncan's unexpired term, Rogers surprised political cynics by winning the race for mayor and carrying a number of other progressive candidates onto the city council with him.[29]

Although he had received important backing from business-progressives, business-developers, and newcomers in the newly annexed areas, Rogers's greatest appeal came from the fact that he was no politician at all. Described by even his political foes as "an honest, decent Christian man" (Kyle Testerman once admitted that Rogers was "cleaner and fresher" than many of his own associates), he was popular with church groups smarting from their recent loss on liquor sales by the bottle, and with business people and others who believed Knoxville needed more imaginative leadership. With a comfortable majority on the city council (despite Walker, who had supported Rogers during the mayoral race but had tried to barter that support for political appointments), Rogers possessed an unmatched opportunity to move Knoxville in new directions.[30]

---

[29]*News-Sentinel*, Mar. 1, 1981.

[30]Interview with Testerman, Jan. 22, 1981. Among Rogers's allies on the city council were Max Friedman, Howard Kesley, W. Dwight Kessel.

Leonard Rogers (third from left)

UT PHOTOGRAPHIC SERVICES

As important to Rogers's victory as the political involvement of new elements was the comparative decline of the old. As noted above, the 1962 annexation had shifted the balance of power toward the middle- and upper-middle-class fringes of the city, which continued to grow at impressive rates. Moreover, the old "floating wards" (principally Wards One, Two, Three, Five, and Seven-S in the center city, where vote-buying was notorious) made up a steadily shrinking proportion of the city's total vote, since the Vine Street–Morningside Heights federal urban renewal project had removed much of the residential housing—and population—from this area. Therefore, what many saw as a political revolution in 1965 actually had been accomplished in part by a demographic revolution. What surprised observers was not so much that the old system had been overturned, but the apparent ease with which it had been done.[31]

Given the constraint of a charter-imposed tax ceiling (which Rogers initially thought politically unwise to challenge), the new mayor's list of accomplishments was impressive. In an attempt to improve the city's bond rating, he employed Wainwright and Ramsey, a professional bond consulting firm from New York, to put together a printed bond prospectus. It was the first time Knoxville had ever done so, and bidders for the important sewer bonds were encouraged. Then, to ease the load on the newly annexed homeowners, he worked out a plan whereby the bonds could be paid off through slight increases in the water bills. Understanding that tax increases had been the undoing of several previous mayors and city managers, Rogers preferred to use further bond issues and increased federal monies to achieve his goals. Three new high schools (Bearden, Central, South-Young) were built in this way, as were the Safety Building, traffic improvements, and the eastern leg of the Downtown Loop. And other ambitious projects were begun, including the new McGhee-Tyson Airport terminal and the Morningside and Mountain View urban renewal projects. If Rogers did not move as boldly as some would have liked, he had acted more energetically than had most of his predecessors.[32]

However, anyone who expected Rogers to be bold simply did not know the man. Having made his reputation as a cautious and judicious (even a trifle conservative, as a result of his rural upbringing) businessman, he was not about to abandon the instincts that had carried him so far. Identifying the principal needs as constructing schools, providing services (especially sewers) for the areas annexed in 1962, and attracting new industries, Rogers moved in a businesslike manner to address these challenges within the constraints imposed by the city charter and by his own personality.[33]

[31]On Gay Way concept see Deaderick, ed., *Heart of the Valley*, 132. On Citizens Group see Baker, "Politics of Innovation," 114. On "floating wards" see *News-Sentinel*, Apr. 19, 1959.

[32]Interview with Leonard Rogers, Jan. 17, 1981; *News-Sentinel*, Mar. 1, 1981.

[33]Interview with Rogers, Jan. 17, 1981.

Rogers's tenure was the longest of any Knoxville mayor to that time since the Civil War. Even so, by the late 1960s his political position had deteriorated badly. Earlier he had fallen out with Cas Walker, at first because Rogers had rejected Walker's patronage demands and later over the sewer financing issue. At the other end of the political spectrum, the business-developer bloc had grown impatient with the mayor's caution and was contemplating running one of its own against Rogers in 1971. Both Walker and the business-developer bloc began undercutting Rogers's position on the council, in an effort to quash his reelection hopes. Walker hammered at Rogers incessantly, hinting darkly of conflicts of interest and undue political pressure on city employees. This pressure was alleged to emanate mostly from the office of Toby Julian, a Rogers appointee whose official duties concerned the city garage but whose primary value to Rogers was as political consultant and wheelhorse. "They beat me to death with Toby Julian," Rogers remembers, "but he was the only man I had who had any political savvy."[34]

Certainly Rogers had little himself. As political opposition mounted, he looked around for those who had urged him to seek the mayoralty in the first place. But they had deserted him, leaving him exposed before the screaming political winds. The business-progressive bloc was an impermanent political coalition at best, its members temperamentally unsuited to the daily demands of politics. Instead, that group preferred, now as in the past, to elect one of its own and then, assured that all was well, retreat to the safety and comfort of its businesses and suburban neighborhoods. Testerman, leader of the business-developer bloc, had already abandoned Rogers and was planning his own campaign to succeed Rogers as mayor. Popular and influential lawyer Claude Robertson, who had been Nixon's Tennessee campaign manager in 1968 and a valuable aide to Rogers in his 1965 victory, was eyeing the governorship and could ill afford to be tied to what appeared to be Rogers's sinking ship. Newcomers who had been annexed in 1962 either had grown impatient with the mayor or had become hopelessly lost in their adopted city's byzantine political intrigues.[35]

Rogers, then, had become a leader without followers. His attempts to overhaul the city police department, which he claimed had been riddled with graft and corruption when he took office (Rogers said later that gambling and prostitution had enriched some police officers), led to charges of a political purge and earned the embattled mayor a host of enemies. His inability to stave off a comparatively modest city property-tax increase was met with howls of rage and anguish and charges of waste. Similar protests met Rogers's scheme to bring in an outside assessor, who would be impervious to local political pressure, to reassess property for revenue purposes. In the

[34]Ibid.; on Julian see *Journal*, Nov. 15, 1971.
[35]Interview with Rogers, Jan. 17, 1981; interview with Testerman, Jan. 22, 1981.

face of these attacks, Rogers seemed strangely paralyzed. "Some of my friends came to me," he remembers, "and told me I ought to go out and campaign in the country clubs. But what would I say to them? I'm a stranger out there."[36]

The end for Rogers came quickly but painfully. Facing Testerman in 1971 in a typically savage Knoxville political campaign, Rogers discovered how untenable his position had become. Testerman's campaign was energetic, well-coordinated, and well-financed, its major theme being that Rogers lacked the vision and energy to get Knoxville moving. Rogers was portrayed (though never by Testerman personally) as a redneck bumpkin, a political naif whose job was simply over his head. Rogers countered that his opponent was a wheeler-dealer, a candidate of the country club group, who would abandon the interests of the majority of the citizens in favor of those of the developers and the "silk-stocking crowd."[37]

Testerman's support of liquor by the drink, his biggest political gamble in 1971, also appeared to influence voters' behavior. Anti-liquor religious groups began leaning toward Rogers, who often mixed religion and politics by campaigning from the pulpits of various local churches. But Testerman made inroads among Knoxville's business and professional newcomers, most of whom believed that the city's drinking ordinances were archaic. As we shall see, for some liquor by the drink had become both symbol and metaphor for Knoxville's modernization.[38]

University faculty members probably supported Testerman, though without much enthusiasm. Many of them had been outraged by Rogers's waffling behavior during the 1970 Billy Graham Crusade in which a number of anti-war students and faculty were arrested when they protested President Nixon's visit to the revival. The charge, disrupting a religious service, was a tenuous one. Police were energetic, though ultimately the penalties were small. Although many UT faculty members viewed Testerman as a cultural barbarian (some of them saw all Knoxville politicians in this light), they supported him partly out of a hope for change and as a reaction against the more conservative Rogers. "If you ever have a chance to choose between Leonard Rogers and a chimpanzee," one of the more liberal members of the faculty blustered, "be sure to make sure which is which."[39]

In reality, Rogers never had a chance. Although he carried the affluent "old money" areas like Sequoyah Hills (where Testerman was seen as a young, arrogant upstart) and some of the older neighborhoods of North Knoxville, he had been badly outmaneuvered by his opponent. Testerman

[36]Interview with Rogers, Jan. 17, 1981.
[37]Ibid. See also *News-Sentinel*, Nov. 1–4, 1971; *Journal*, Nov. 1–4, 11, 17, 1971.
[38]Interview with Rogers, Jan. 17, 1981.
[39]Ibid.

*Dr. Billy Graham and President Richard Nixon
at the Knoxville Crusade, May 1970*

REPRINTED FROM *Billy Graham in Big Orange Country*
WITH THE PERMISSION OF MR. RALPH FROST

had won Cas Walker's endorsement and, while that was not the political prize it once had been, that support probably helped him among the black and working-class white voters. More important, Testerman carried the populous newer West Knoxville suburbs, the "floating wards" of Mechan- icsville, and a large share of the business community. Though the typically vicious campaign would leave deep scars, Kyle Testerman began his admin- istration with a clear-cut electoral victory in the runoff.[40]

An embittered Leonard Rogers vacated the mayor's office, taking a posi- tion with the UT Institute for Public Service. And even by the time of his early retirement ten years later (in 1981), the bitterness had not totally evaporated. Lampooned by his political foes and deserted by his allies, he felt that the city had failed to appreciate the progress he had made. And perhaps it had. For the Rogers years (1965–1971) were important ones in redirecting Knoxville away from its troubled past and into new channels. If Rogers did not create all the forces responsible for this redirection, at least he knew how to use them judiciously. Indeed, if anyone can be credited for laying the groundwork for what was to come, Rogers clearly can. Ironically, although he was elected in 1965 principally because he was not a politician, ultimately that fact proved his undoing.[41]

In many ways Kyle Testerman was the opposite of Leonard Rogers. Physically, Testerman resembled a professional football player toward the end of his career (the thirty-six-year-old mayor actually was a fine tennis player), whereas Rogers might well have been mistaken for a small-town bank president who preferred a quiet game of horseshoes. The new mayor had grown up in Knoxville in comparative opulence, while Rogers could not disguise his modest rural background. Testerman favored well-tailored, expensive clothes and the latest fashions (including body jewelry); Rogers dressed modestly. Testerman was bold in personality and vocabulary, whereas Rogers was almost shy. Indeed, no better symbols of the aggressive business-developer and the more conservative and cautious business- progressive could be found than Kyle Testerman and Leonard Rogers.

But the difference between the two men went far beyond surface impres- sions. Rogers lacked political acumen, whereas Testerman was more sagacious. In a comparatively short time, the new mayor had accumulated a massive amount of local political knowledge. He knew who had real power and who did not, who held the strings and where they led ("On the school board, Sarah Moore Greene wouldn't go to the bathroom until she'd checked with Cas Walker"),[42] who could deliver the votes and who could not, who knew where the political bodies were buried and who did not. By

[40]*Journal*, Nov. 5, 1971. For runoff results see ibid., Nov. 19, 1971.
[41]Interview with Rogers, Jan. 17, 1981; *News-Sentinel*, Mar. 1, 1981.
[42]Interview with Testerman, Jan. 22, 1981.

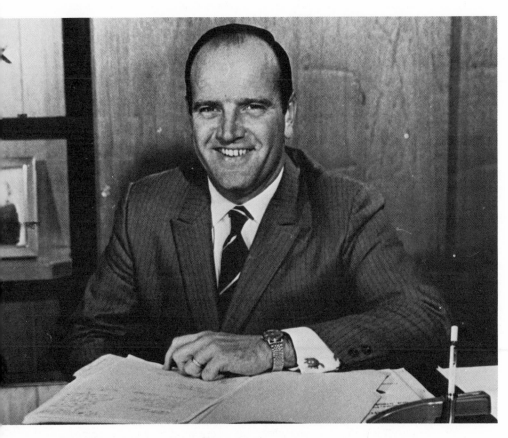

Kyle Testerman

<small>KNOXVILLE</small> *News-Sentinel*

the time he came to be head of the business-developer bloc and unseated Rogers in 1971, Testerman was one of the most knowledgeable political figures in the city's modern history.

Nor did Testerman lack well-thought-out- goals and bold dreams. To him the time for planning and debate was over. Realizing, as a developer would, that downtown Knoxville would never again become the region's retail shopping center, Testerman conceived of the downtown area as a business-financial district. "It's a national trend," he mused, "and even Rich's couldn't fight it." Following Knoxville's "1990 Plan," a development plan created while he was on the MPC in 1970, Testerman envisioned the Gay Street area as the business-financial district. West of that would be a major north-south outdoor mall development, bounded by the TVA towers on the north and a new city-county building on the south. An east-west mall, mixing exclusive new townhouses, pedestrian walkways, and specialty shops would intersect the Market Street Mall.[43]

If Knoxville were to achieve those ambitious plans, the new mayor believed, two things had to happen. First, federal funds from revenue-sharing and community-development grants had to be attracted, and attracted in a magnitude that Knoxville had never seen before. Second, new private money had to be lured downtown. "One of the things that held Knoxville back," the developer-mayor explained, "was that a high proportion of downtown property was controlled by a small number of old-money families. For downtown development to take place, those old estates had to be broken up. Private money could do a lot of that, but I'd use the power of eminent domain if necessary."[44]

Indeed, the new mayor seemed almost daily to explode with new ideas. Only thirty-six years old when he became mayor, Testerman brought into city hall with him an aggressive and innovative group of young people, some barely out of college. There were a few, such as Guy Smith IV (press secretary), who had political ties to some of the old power groups, but most were a new breed of apolitical managers whose brainstorming sessions went on well into the night and whose days were spent trying to implement their schemes. Men like Darcy Sullivan, Steve Blackwell, Jim Easton, Robert Booker, Graham Hunter, Mike Hill, Buddy Palmore, Louis Hofferbert, and others may have had little political clout, but they had something more valuable in the awakening city: access to Testerman, whose political savvy and flamboyance both stimulated and publicized their dreams.[45]

Luckily, the money was there. A combination of aggressive and imagina-

---

[43]Metropolitan Planning Commission and East Tennessee Development District, *General Plan, 1990* (Knoxville, 1970); interview with Testerman, Jan. 22, 1981.

[44]Interview with Testerman, Jan. 22, 1981.

[45]Interview with Guy Smith IV, Dec. 29, 1981.

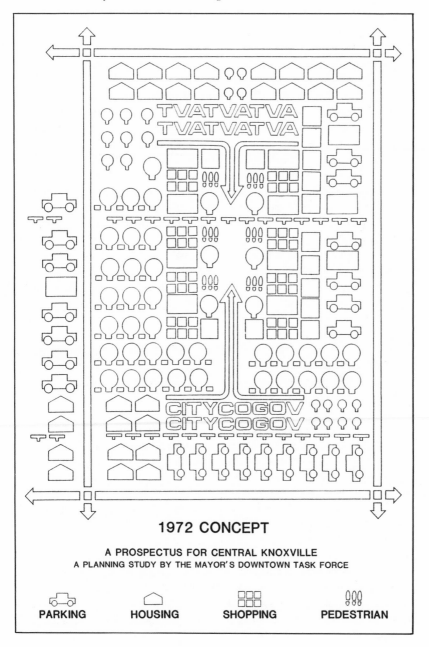

VII. Downtown Concept Map, 1972

tive grant-proposal writing and wily political horse trading with the Nixon administration secured about $84 million in revenue-sharing and community-development money. Money was acquired for the TVA twin towers, the city-county building, the Bicentennial Park, and the double mall. In a major downtown cleanup effort (dubbed "Bury City Hall"), tons of garbage were collected from streets and alleys by private citizens and dumped on the steps of City Hall. In truth, it seems as if Testerman could make good his boast that he was going to "bulldoze downtown and start all over again."[46]

In his campaign against Rogers, Testerman had vowed to liberalize the city's liquor laws. Though few could vouch for their veracity, there were oft-told stories of convention business that Knoxville had lost because it did not allow the sale of liquor by the drink. But referenda on that issue (the most recent in 1966) had failed before, killed (it was rumored) by a strange combination of church groups and liquor dealer interests, and by the apathy of those who belonged to private clubs where they could evade the spirit of the law while drinking as they pleased. Finally in 1961 (on the third try in seven years) a liquor-by-the-bottle referendum had passed, largely because private clubs were being raided and bootlegger sources drying up. But in the meantime other southern cities had passed liquor-by-the-drink referenda and, presumably because of that, had seen an upswing in their convention business.

Testerman threw his full weight on the side of change. First, he secured a separate city referendum (previously, county and city had voted together on this issue, and the county vote had been strongly anti-liberalization). Then the mayor visited every private club in the city, vowing to close all of them down the day after the vote if the referendum failed. Hoping for convention dollars as well as potential new hotel construction, much of the business community went along. The result was a triumph for Testerman: the 1972 liquor-by-the-drink referendum passed by more than two to one. Fittingly, the first legal drink was mixed for and consumed by the ebullient mayor at Ireland's Restaurant on Cumberland Avenue. Trivia buffs may note that it was a gin and tonic, which Testerman, never famous as a teetotaler, consumed with ill-disguised satisfaction.[47]

The event was thoroughly symbolic. For the first time since the World War I era, when Mayor John E. McMillan had stood against overt racism and the Ku Klux Klan, a Knoxville mayor had broken with traditional local mores and had cast his political lot with the demographic future. Testerman willingly proclaimed Halloween 1972 as 'Trick or Treat for UNICEF Eve," ignoring the fact that but a few years earlier Knoxvillians had argued over

[46]Ibid.
[47]Baker, "Politics of Innovation," 73, 97.

whether that organization was communistic or not (Mayors Duncan and Rogers had both called such a proclamation "political dynamite"). Testerman proposed the trial consolidation of city and county schools, despite warnings that the always-dangerous issue of racial integration lurked not far below the surface. He openly castigated the elected school board as timid, interest-ridden, and shortsighted. His occasionally colorful speech, reminiscent of Harry Truman's on his saltier days, drew both gasps and sympathetic laughter in just about equal doses. His immediate embrace of the world's fair concept earned him both praise and condemnation. Indeed, it was as if the mayor's office was too staid and confining, almost suffocating, for this young, athletic man. His ideas and energy seemed almost boundless, and he appeared to want to offer new and innovative ideas even before his older ones had been brought to fruition.[48]

As Rogers before him had been, Testerman was aided by a number of fortuitous circumstances. The University of Tennessee, which had expanded to approximately 26,000 students, now had an enormous payroll and almost inexhaustible construction money. By the mid-1970s the Blount Mansion Historic Area was completed, and the restoration of the famous Lamar House–Bijou Theater was underway. The Hyatt-Regency hotel was about to see the light at the end of their profit-and-loss tunnel. The Summit Hill Project was well underway, "opening up" the northern section of downtown and providing a future connector into the Fort Sanders–University of Tennessee area. Federal money continued to flow, and the entertainment and liquor taxes were providing needed revenue, even generating the luxury of a budget surplus and property tax decreases from time to time. Indeed, it seemed as if all was well.

But for Testerman all was not well. His impatience with the normally languid processes of government, his open contempt of those who disagreed with him, his reputation as a wheeler-dealer developer, and his willingness to take positions on even the most controversial issues in the end overwhelmed him. Perhaps he wanted Knoxville to change too rapidly; he wanted the city, after decades of inertia, to be remade overnight. In 1975, in a reelection bid, he failed to secure a majority on the first ballot and was forced into a runoff with the popular Randy Tyree. Testerman was stunned, bewildered, hurt, and angry. In an ill-advised election eve outburst that was widely covered by television reporters, he lashed out at the voters whom he believed had betrayed him. Tyree won the runoff, principally by carrying North and South Knoxville where voters were largely white middle-class and blue-collar workers. While Testerman won in East Knoxville (mostly black voters) and West Knoxville (upper-middle-class business-professional

---

[48]Interview with Smith, Dec. 29, 1981.

and prosperous newcomers), the heavy turnout in the older and more populous northern and southern areas of the city overwhelmed him.[49]

Looking back on his defeat, Testerman believes himself to have been a victim of the Watergate backlash that turned out incumbents throughout the nation. And he may be more correct than he realizes. Though the two men are vastly different, to some it appeared that Richard Nixon had a local counterpart. Moreover, Testerman's young staff seemed too much like local versions of Haldeman, Erlichman, Ziegler, and Dean, men of the new, nonideological, almost apolitical managerial class. In some ways they probably were.[50]

But to see Testerman as a victim of the backlash against Nixon is simplistic. The mayor's liquor-by-the-drink stand had alienated large portions of the city. Many felt he was too favorable to developers, substantial businessmen, and newcomers. His comments on school consolidation had earned him few friends. His early falling-out with Cas Walker gave him an enemy who even as late as 1975 could not be underrated. Finally, his effective but comparatively brutal breaking of a strike by municipal garbage collectors (later Testerman was to brag about how he had so frightened a union organizer from out of town that the man had left the city) shocked unions and liberals, especially around the university. In sum, Kyle Testerman had made too many political enemies, had given and taken too many political wounds, had shown himself too contemptuous of the average voters for them to support him any longer.

One must not, however, overlook the fact that Testerman's principal opponent in his 1975 reelection bid was an attractive and popular candidate. Indeed, in many ways Randy Tyree was everything Testerman was not. Born in 1940 in Smith County, Tyree was the son of a sharecropper and had known poverty from the beginning. Fiercely ambitious and determined to rise from his humble origins, he joined the FBI after graduating from high school, starting in the records section and working his way up to field investigator. Realizing that his lack of a college education prevented him from rising further, Tyree enrolled at Middle Tennessee State University in 1962, graduated in three years, and then entered the University of Tennessee Law School, from which he was graduated in 1967. His love of police work, his FBI experience, and his recently acquired education made him an asset to the Knoxville police department, where he specialized in undercover operations aimed at reversing the city's growing narcotics traffic. In 1969 he first came to the public's attention with Operation Aquarius, a massive roundup of drug pushers principally in the UT area. In 1971 he became Leonard

[49]Ibid.; *News-Sentinel*, Nov. 21, 1975.

[50]Interview with Testerman, Jan. 22, 1981.

[51]On strike see interview with Testerman, Jan. 22, 1981.

Randy Tyree

KNOXVILLE *News-Sentinel*

Rogers's safety director, resigning when Testerman asked him to do so in January 1972. On that date, according to his critics, he began his four-year campaign for mayor. Unsullied by the city's often fetid political trenches, Tyree radiated modesty, decency, a self-deprecating humor, and sincerity (one of his critics said, "He can look at you with those sincere blue eyes and lie to you and you come out *believing* him").[52]

To blue-collar workers in North and South Knoxville, Tyree was one of their own. Even though many had sons and daughters attending UT, they often saw that place as a haven for radicals, drugs, and unwholesome sexual activity, and Tyree's role in Operation Aquarius gained him many supporters. Loyal supporters of Leonard Rogers backed Tyree as a form of retaliation against Testerman. Tyree's initial stand on what was to become the World's Fair (to be discussed below) led critics of that project to believe they had a friend in him. Finally, those North and South Knoxvillians who believed Testerman was "giving too much" to West Knoxville and had placed the city's government in the hands of greedy developers supported Tyree.

In all, however, probably Testerman's greatest foe was his own style. In a city that had just awakened from decades of virtual slumber, he pushed too hard, moved too fast, advocated too many changes at once for a populace used to more judicious and conservative political leadership. In the end it was his undoing.

So the political days of Rogers and Testerman, who both had done so much to rejuvenate and redirect the ailing city, ended similarly in defeat and bitterness. Rogers had been a casualty of his own cautiousness and political innocence, Testerman of his own reckless courage and political style. Interestingly, both saw the solutions to Knoxville's problems as coming from outside the city, from new private money, from newly arrived residents, from Washington agencies. Both seemed to believe that Knoxville itself lacked the resources and the will to effect major changes in its character. Rogers sought to deal with political reactionaries by demonstrating how sound, conservative business techniques could effect great wonders, whereas Testerman tried simply to kick his political opposition to death. In the end both suffered the same fate, one as a result of local factionalism and the other as a victim of a genuine political uprising.

And despite some of the most dramatic changes the city had ever seen, one is forced to wonder whether in truth anything had changed at all. More properly put, had either Rogers or Testerman been able to harness the forces that in the 1960s and 1970s had buffeted nearly every American city? Rogers, the older of the two men, had tried to use the methods that had

[52]On four-year campaign, see interview with Smith, Dec. 29, 1981. On one critic's view of Tyree's apparent sincerity, see conversation with Dr. Joe Dodd, Mar. 24, 1979.

succeeded for him in business, without fully appreciating the magnitude of the forces he faced. For his part, Testerman understood those forces better and was less beholden to traditional solutions. But the forces of demography and history appear to have been too powerful for either man to withstand or conquer.

MALL FEVER, DOWNTOWN, AND THE "QUANTUM JUMP"

For one thing, the continuing waves of affluent newcomers, mostly business and professional people, tended to settle in the new developments along the western axis. By the early 1970s the population center of Knox County had shifted westward to approximately the area of the new Bearden High School, roughly ten miles from the center city. In the Rocky Hill–Bluegrass area alone, between 1960 and 1968 population jumped an astounding 69 percent. A large proportion of these newcomers settled west of the city limits, depriving the city of needed tax revenues. More important, these newcomers tended to form attitudinal enclaves of their own, hence deepening the chasm between them and the older residents of the city. Generally younger, better educated, and more liberal in their social views (dramatized by the liquor issue, for example), less tied to traditional ideas, more accustomed to demanding educational and social services, and more inclined to organize themselves into homeowners' and issues-oriented groups, these men and women made the story of Knoxville truly a tale of two cities.[53]

As we have seen, the downtown had received a needed facelift in the late 1960s. But affluent newcomers rarely came downtown to shop, preferring instead the easy accessibility and spacious, free parking of the shopping malls which in the 1970s had sprung up all along Kingston Pike. The Chrysler Corporation had started this boom in the late 1960s by constructing West Town Mall in the Bearden area. Chrysler soon sold the almost-completed project to other interests, but the mall boom had begun. By 1978, every movie theater in downtown Knoxville was closed, while over ten had opened in the west. Restaurants, except for the well-established and twice-renovated Regas, generally suffered, and downtown retail business was uneven at best. As Testerman and the Center City Task Force recognized, if downtown Knoxville was to be revitalized as a retail trade area (and Testerman was dubious on that score), then major residential projects would have to be undertaken to lure affluent newcomers to the center city.

But no major residential development took place in the downtown area. Instead, city consumers and taxpayers in the 1960s and 1970s increasingly tended to be elderly, black, and poor, or living on fixed incomes severely

[53]*News-Sentinel*, Nov. 26, 1968.

threatened by the national inflation of the Vietnam and post-Vietnam eras. By 1970 over 11 percent of Knoxville's population was sixty-five and over, and approximately 30,000 (17 percent) people lived on fixed incomes. In spite of some rather massive urban renewal projects, the city's blacks continued to live in depressed conditions, which became breeding grounds for social problems. A 1973 study, done by the Knoxville–Knox County Community Action Committee (of which Testerman was the vice-chairman), showed that city planning units with high proportions of black residents led the city in school dropouts, infant mortality, tuberculosis, venereal disease, adult arrests, juvenile delinquency, and public assistance.[54]

For the city government the problem was clear. The center city, largely inhabited by the poor, the black, and the elderly, continued to demand services that took more money to provide than the city collected in tax revenues from this area. At the same time, an increasing proportion of affluent newcomers were settling west of the city limits (the Farragut–Cedar Bluff area was becoming virtually one enormous suburban development), were not returning downtown to shop, and were luring retail businesses away from the city and into the malls. Should the city government continue to chase and envelop these people and businesses on the western rimland? If so, was continued annexation or a countywide metropolitan government (similar to Nashville's area) the easiest and most efficient method? In short, if the people that Knoxville wanted would not come to the city, then should the city go to them? And how would these people react to this blatant but understandable urban imperialism?

Last, reliance on continued injections of federal and state dollars was at best naive and at worst foolish. Testerman had presided over Knoxville in the days when federal grants had been large and readily available. But in the mid-1970s, toward the end of Testerman's administration, it was already becoming clear that the flow of federal-, state-, and university-induced money could not go on forever. UT had expanded to the limits of its classroom and dormitory space, and any future growth would take massive capital outlays—funds the state simply did not have. Federal and state money continued, but inflation diminished its buying power. Harried public school officials looked for programs to cut and were even forced to consider slicing academic as well as extracurricular programs. Parents' groups campaigning for new programs, such as regular physical education or foreign languages at the elementary school level, found themselves swimming against the tide.

But if the problem was clear, the solution was less so. Concerned business people and developers increasingly talked of a "quantum jump" needed

---

[54]Knoxville–Knox County Community Action Committee, *Poverty in Knoxville and Knox County* (Knoxville, 1973), 23.

Shopping Centers and Large Discount Stores

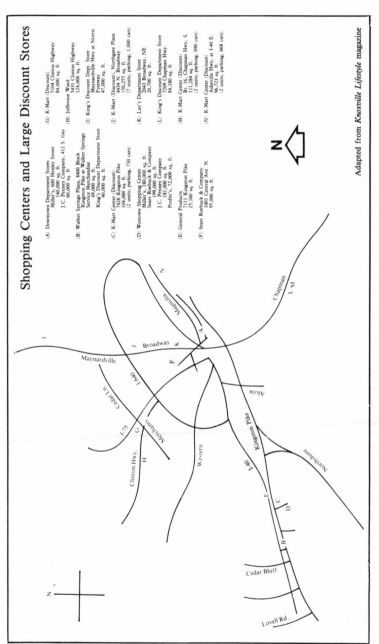

(A) Downtown Department Stores
Miller's, 600 Henley Street
140,000 sq. ft.
J.C. Penney Company, 412 S. Gay
60,000 sq. ft.

(B) Walker Springs Plaza, 8400 Block
Kingston Pike at Walker Springs
Service Merchandise
49,000 sq. ft.
King's Discount Department Store
40,000 sq. ft.

(C) K-Mart Center (Discount)
7428 Kingston Pike
104,000 sq. ft.
(2 units, parking, 730 cars)

(D) Westtown Shopping Center
Miller's, 180,000 sq. ft.
Sears Roebuck & Company
199,000 sq. ft.
J.C. Penney Company
181,000 sq. ft.
Profit's, 72,000 sq. ft.

(E) General Products
7111 Kingston Pike
25,160 sq. ft.

(F) Sears Roebuck & Company
1001 Central Ave. N.
95,000 sq. ft.

(G) K-Mart (Discount)
5104 Clinton Highway
84,000 sq. ft.

(H) Jefferson Ward
5431 Clinton Highway
124,000 sq. ft.

(I) King's Discount Dept. Store
Maynardville Hwy at Norris
Freeway
47,000 sq. ft.

(J) K-Mart (Discount) Northgate Plaza
4434 N. Broadway
150,255 sq. ft.
(7 units; parking, 1,000 cars)

(K) Lay's Department Store
2043 Broadway, NE
20,700 sq. ft.

(L) King's Discount Department Store
7209 Chapman Hwy.
84,180 sq. ft

(M) K-Mart Center (Discount)
Rt. 16, Chapman Hwy. S.
111,284 sq. ft.
(2 units; parking, 690 cars)

(N) K-Mart Center (Discount)
Asheville Hwy., at I-40 E.
96,773 sq. ft.
(2 units, parking, 668 cars)

Adapted from Knoxville *Lifestyle* magazine

VIII. *Shopping Centers and Major Department Stores*

to revitalize downtown, get construction rolling again, continue to attract massive amounts of public money, lure tourist dollars (one city official jokingly proposed inventing a machine to "stop tourists going to the Smoky Mountains at the city limits, turn them upside down and shake some money out of them"), and increase city revenues. Before long, the term "quantum jump" was on the lips of many merchants and government officials.

They knew what they wanted to do. In the early 1970s the Boeing Corporation had sent planners to the region for the purpose of building a new city, to be named Timberlake, near the Tellico Dam (which was under construction). From the beginning, the TVA Tellico Dam project had been surrounded by controversy, and although the Knoxville city council under Leonard Rogers had endorsed the project, many Knoxvillians opposed the dam as unnecessary, wasteful, an exercise in self-justification by TVA, and harmful to the environment. Lawsuits by environmentalists, including a famous suit to preserve a small fish called the snail darter by placing it on the endangered species list, blocked the development of Timberlake. Finding the Boeing planners in Knoxville with nothing to do, Mayor Testerman convinced the giant corporation to lend the planners to the city at no cost. The result was a General Redevelopment Plan, adopted by the city council in 1972. The plan was a bold one. It proposed opening up downtown to massive mall-like developments and residences, overcoming the topographical features that separated UT from the CBD, and incorporating massive amounts of accessible parking space. But developers, business people, and political figures still bemoaned the lack of the "quantum jump" necessary to translate the plan into reality. Testerman could get grants, start public buildings, cajole downtown property owners, and use the powers of eminent domain. However, even that would not be enough.[55]

On a trip to Tulsa in 1974, W. Stewart Evans, a retired military officer and president of the DKA, had happened to meet King Cole, the man who had developed an international exposition in Spokane, Washington. Returning to Knoxville aflame like one saved at a revival meeting, Evans broadly announced, "I've found our quantum jump—a world's fair in Knoxville!"[56] Mayor Testerman, hardly one to think small, was immediately excited and suggested banker Jake Butcher to head a committee charged with doing a feasibility study. Though Testerman and Butcher were not close (perhaps their egos and political ambitions made close friendship impossible), Butcher was an ideal choice, for he not only gave the scheme a bipartisan character (he had already sought the Democratic nomination for governor

---

[55] On Knoxville city council's endorsement of the Tellico Dam, see *News-Sentinel*, July 14, 1965.

[56] Address by George Siler, Univ. of Tennessee, Aug. 15, 1979; address by Carroll Logan, Univ. of Tennessee, July 8, 1980.

Jake Butcher

KNOXVILLE *News-Sentinel*

once and was considering doing so again), but he also had a boldness of mind to match Testerman's and considerable financial leverage. The Knoxville International Energy Exposition, Inc. (KIEE, a private, nonprofit organization) was formed in early 1976. The Bureau of International Expositions (BIE) in Paris was contacted, and Evans (with the combined power of Testerman and Butcher behind him) began drumming up public support.

Although a number of sites for the exposition were considered, in reality only one site fit the Boeing plan: the lower Second Creek area, a parcel of roughly 70 acres running south from Western Avenue, in the corridor between the university and downtown. Once called Scuffletown, for years the valley had been the scene of slum dwellings around the Southern Railway yard that bisected the valley. By 1972 most of the houses had been torn down. Since UT moved to its present campus, the area had effectively separated the campus from the downtown. In the Boeing plan, this area was immensely important, both for "reconnecting" UT with downtown and for establishing residential housing and parking near the center city.

Needing a theme to present to the BIE, planners settled on that of "Energy Turns the World," hoping that UT and Oak Ridge connections might attract "new, high-tech" energy-related industries to Knoxville after the 184-day exposition. Later, George Siler, the exposition's executive vice-president, admitted that the "energy theme was a fluke that just fell in our laps." But the *real* theme was the redevelopment of Knoxville, the "quantum jump" many felt was so necessary.[57]

Essentially, then, the project was a private enterprise clothed in the garb of a public institution. The city (through the KCDC) acquired the land and prepared the site, using an $11.6-million city bond issue for money. "The city now owns the land," said exposition president S.H. (Bo) Roberts, "and will use it after the fair to continue the redevelopment project, converting it to recreational, residential and commercial uses."[58]

The Spokane World's Fair had been held over the objections of a majority of voters in a local referendum on whether to undertake the project. Evans, Testerman, and Butcher—who probably feared that innate conservative feelings, combined with suspicion of "outsiders" and aversion to any tax increases, would stop Expo in its tracks—had no intention of holding such a referendum. Instead, they tried to woo the citizens with artists' renderings of highway improvements and visions of tourist dollars, while staving off calls for a referendum. Randy Tyree, who had defeated Testerman for mayor in 1975 and had exhibited a neutrality toward Expo that some voters had misinterpreted as hostility, swung into line in 1976. Together with the city council, Tyree shut off moves for a referendum, while the date of Expo (to

[57]Address by Siler, Aug. 15, 1979.
[58]*The Tennessee Alumnus*, LXI (Fall 1981), 6.

be called the World's Fair when the BIE gave its final imprimatur) was set at 1982 and the KCDC began acquiring property. A combination of federal, state, and private money, much of it extracted by the powerful Butcher, began to trickle in.

Private polls showed the fair's opponents to be a curious mixture of old and new Knoxville. Cas Walker initially was adamantly opposed, singing his old song to his old constituency about higher taxes and huge profits for the "silk-stocking crowd." But many professional people and affluent newcomers were opposed also, fearing that their "peaceful little city" would be the scene of massive traffic congestion and a cheap carnival atmosphere. University political science professor Joe Dodd, a leader of the movement to block Expo, hinted darkly of poor planning, underfinancing, and probable financial failure. But the city council and the mayor's office were too strong for the opponents and had too many resources for the anti-Expo forces. Walker gradually lessened his opposition, and Dodd lost ground as the pro-Expo coalition wore him down.[59]

Indeed, if anything, many Knoxvillians came to see the World's Fair and its aftereffects (dubbed "residuals" by fair promoters and supporters) as the answer to all the city's problems. In this, the World's Fair officials were in part culpable. While they always added the caveat that the ambitious project could not do all things for all people, their responses to attacks and criticisms tended to emphasize the notion that the 1982 World's Fair would "turn the city around."

Writing in the winter of 1981–1982, the authors would not be so bold as to predict whether the World's Fair will be a success or whether the residuals of the fair will be all its hopeful boosters claim for them. What we *can* do, however, is to identify the problems facing the city, problems that are in large part rooted in Knoxville's history, its culture, and its collective mentality. In truth, what we *are* saying is that those who see the World's Fair as the "quantum jump" necessary for the city to move successfully into the postindustrial age must realize that they expect the fair and its residuals to reverse historical trends of long standing.

Of prime importance to fair supporters is the revival of the inner city. That is a truly formidable task. For almost one-half a century, the old Knoxville (the pre-1962 city) has declined by almost every statistical indicator. Clearly, it is the poorest area of the city. While average family income for Knoxville as a whole in 1977 was $11,190 (and for Sequoyah Hills

[59] For opposition to Expo see *News-Sentinel*, June 1, 1979; Leon Ridenour (Chair, Citizens for a Better Knoxville) to John Cole (Regional Environmentalist, Economic Development Administration), June 11, 1979, copy in possession of authors; Joe Dodd, *Expo Time Schedule* (mass reproduced broadside, 1979, in possession of authors); Joe Dodd, Public Hearing Mar. 24, 1979, Regional Urban Design Assistance Team Hearings, held at St. John's Episcopal Church.

$34,562), the inner-city census tracts of Beaumont ($5,660), Mountain View ($6,486), and Broadway ($7,542) were well below that average. That trend is a strong one that, to be reversed, would take a good deal of ingenuity and money.[60]

As one would expect, accompanying the inner city's problem of poverty are massive social problems as well. Of the twenty-three planning units in 1975, the eight inner-city planning units that ranked lowest in family incomes were also the areas that ranked highest in social disorders (venereal disease, infant mortality, tuberculosis, school dropouts, adult arrests, and aid to dependent children). Those units were Mountain View, Beaumont, Lonsdale, East Knoxville, CBD, Broadway, Vestal, and Sharp's Ridge. Nor were these areas simply poor black enclaves. One of Beaumont's three census tracts contained the highest percentage (53.2 percent) of poor in the city, yet was but 7.9 percent black. Simply put, these are the remnants of yesterday's people in today's city.[61]

Many believe that the revival of the inner city rests on the ability to attract comparatively young, wealthy, childless married couples to live in the inner city (young and wealthy in terms of consumption patterns and childless in terms of the unwillingness to expand neighborhood educational and recreation facilities). The 1977 Regional Urban Development Assistance Team (RUDAT) reported that creating this type of inner-city residential housing was an absolute necessity. Yet, unlike many other urban areas (where inner-city housing stock was essentially brick and therefore durable), Knoxville's inner-city housing has decayed badly. Nor do the very people the city seeks to attract to the inner city show much interest in being pioneers on this new downtown frontier. Indeed, the August 1981 MPC study *Knoxville's Center City* reported that "a significant middle-upper class 'back-to-the-city' movement has yet to develop." The efforts of "gentrification" being made in the Fourth and Gill neighborhood of old North Knoxville and at Christopher Kendrick's Masonic Square may be wedges of a new trend and a reversal of suburban flight, but it is too early to tell whether they are pioneers or lone outposts.[62]

In addition, those who see the revival of the inner city as a regional retail center are hoping, in the face of all available evidence, that "mall fever" has spent itself and that the downtown will gradually be reestablished—with the help of the World's Fair—as a primary retail shopping area. They count on

---

[60]Income by census tract, obtained from MPC, 1979.

[61]MPC, *Poverty in Knoxville and Knox County* (Knoxville, Jan. 1976), 20.

[62]For remark on "back-to-the-city movement" see UT Graduate School of Planning Research Center, "A Housing Market Study for Lower Second Creek Redevelopment Plan," quoted in MPC, *Knoxville's Center City: Data and Technical Information Report* (Knoxville, Aug. 1981), 14. For RUDAT report see *After Expo* (Knoxville, Mar. 1979).

retail trade generated (largely during the lunch hour) by those working in the city's new downtown office complexes. Yet, as office buildings continue to change Knoxville's downtown skyline, retail trade continues to slip. By 1977 the center city's share of the SMSA's retail sales was less than half of what it had been in 1967, a staggering loss given inflation. And "mall fever" shows no sign of stopping, with the East Town Mall already under construction northeast of the inner city.[63]

Even the dreams of the reestablishment of the downtown as a major office center may be illusory. Although the CBD has declined proportionately in retail trade, this trend has been partially offset by the city's shift to the service sector of the economy from the industrial, a move that has caused office space to be an important economic factor. Office use is the fastest growing land use in the CBD. Between 1974 and 1981 nearly $140,000,000 was invested in new office building and renovation in fourteen separate projects. These projects included the nearly $32-million city-county building, the $30 million TVA towers, and the United American Plaza (nearly $27 million). Almost 3 million square feet of office space and two parking garages were the result of this spurt of growth, but current (1982) proposals project nearly 2 million square feet more, a projected rate of growth that to those who feel that office space has stabilized appears serenely optimistic.[64]

Many of the desirable businesses sought by the CBD are heavy employers of support staffs which have located in the fastest growing residential areas of the further western and northern axes of the city. It is unlikely that as transportation and parking costs mount, the inner city will be more attractive to these types of firms than the areas to the west and north of the city within convenient reach of their employees. It may well be that nonretail businesses can follow the tendency of retail trade to group themselves in smaller modules around the city rather than locating in the CBD, a tendency that current postindustrial innovations in communication are likely to enhance.

CBD projects of more than $300,000 in estimated new construction costs grew enormously in 1974, peaking at over $12 million (TVA towers) and leapt again in 1975 (city-county building) and 1977 (UAB Plaza). By 1980, World's Fair–related projects had driven estimated construction costs over $300,000 to $26 million, and the first six months of 1981 topped out at nearly $37 million of investment, which constituted 93.4 percent of the CBD development. The Holiday Inn, exhibition hall, and office building alone accounted for $20 million of this.[65] Can the city sustain, *after* the fair, enough operational revenue to sustain four major downtown hotels, where before the fair there was one (Hyatt-Regency)?

---

[63] For slippage of CBD share of retail trade see MPC, *Knoxville's Center City*, 124–25.
[64] Ibid., 9–10, 12, 16.
[65] Ibid., 9–10.

Inasmuch as buildings like the TVA towers and the UAB Plaza account for peaks in the investment schedule in the CBD, so too they account for an inordinate contribution to the CBD tax distribution. In fact, TVA towers, UAB Plaza, Park National Bank, Summit Hill towers, and Summer Place garage (TVA) account for just over 50 percent of the CBD tax yield. The last countywide appraisal was in 1972, and the years 1975, 1977, 1979, and 1980 have seen a steadily falling ratio of appraised values to true market value, which in 1975 was 75 percent but in 1980 was 49.6 percent. A projected appraisal in 1983 will raise, it is expected, the taxes and the revenue. Tax yield in the CBD is not only badly distributed and underassessed, but 31.8 percent of the CBD is land that is tax exempt. Held mainly by the KCDC, it will yield taxes once, if ever, developed. Ten blocks of the CBD are tax exempt, forty-nine blocks pay less than $100,000 annually, and only three blocks (TVA towers, UAB Plaza, Park National Bank) pay in excess of $200,000 annually.[66]

If office space has stabilized—and one must keep in mind that much new space caused the then-occupied space to be vacated (TVA especially)—can inner-city residential growth make up the balance? After the World's Fair, will enough residual residential use of the World's Fair site occur? One of the more striking features of the selection of Knoxville as a World's Fair site has been the impetus to finish badly needed adjustments in the downtown interstate access (malfunction junction) and to complete the beltway connection between I-40 West and I-75 North—the I-640 connector. The result of many of these improvements has been, or will be, better, easier, and faster access to the inner city and out of it. Hence, even if much of the projected office space is built and occupied, the improved transportation network may make it desirable to remain in the western and northern suburbs and commute into the CBD. Ironically, the fair may have worked to retard any movement into the inner city for residential purposes.

Residential housing in the World's Fair site, a logical place for a revitalization movement of downtown to begin, is difficult to project. Most certainly in this era of Reaganomics it will not be federally subsidized urban housing, and yet there is reason to doubt that Knoxville has the kind and size of population to sustain a real inner-city residential renaissance, which is generally reckoned to consist of condominiums starting well in excess of $80,000.

The old Knoxville and the future Knoxville confront one another across a chasm. Any of us can drive to the World's Fair site and speculate about the success of the fair itself and the residuals—in this sense the future appears more visible to us than the past, because, though we drive through the old industrial Knoxville every day on interstates, we lose sight of our history, because the highways have cut wide swaths through what were recognizable

---

[66]Ibid., 24, 121–22.

and tangible neighborhoods. This is tragic on many accounts. We have become visually separated from our own past. The bifurcation that exists and has historically existed among us is masked at precisely the time when we, as a city, most need the sense of what we have been.

Knoxvillians may expect the 1982 World's Fair, for all its obvious benefits, to do too much. In 1981 David Stockman, President Reagan's director of the Office of Management and Budget, remarked, "When you have powerful underlying demographic and economic forces at work, federal intervention efforts designed to reverse the tide turn out to have rather anemic effects." Many Knoxvillians hope that the World's Fair and its residuals will prove Stockman wrong. For Knoxville, the jury is still out.[67]

Of course, the other alternative (the one implied by Stockman) is to allow demographic and economic forces to go on unchallenged or unarrested. For some, "the answer" is to build new cities, cities with no poor, no undered- ucated, no unskilled, no outmoded industries or enterprises, no outmoded housing stock, no ugliness, no urban blight. For those utopians, "the an- swer" is to "start all over again."

But that dream, seductive as it might be, is an unrealistic one. For one thing, that dream would remove Knoxville from Appalachia, the region that has been the source of so many of the city's opportunities and problems. Knoxville, Tennessee, is an Appalachian city, a city that chose to follow the New South rainbow and for that both has prospered and has paid. Moreover, that seductive dream of the utopian city is a dream that ignores the human dimension of what a city is and what it does. Those dreamers expect the ultimate, that a city can cut itself off from its history and its historical function.

In some ways Knoxville has escaped its own history, but in many ways it has not. No longer a sleepy little town on a new railroad, it has become a modern city, sharing the opportunities and problems of all modern cities. Those who would have returned to the sleepy village could not; those who would have seen Knoxville unmoved in its present, suspended in time, could not. Knoxville's future, however, will surely be no less comfortable and no more troubled than its uncomfortable and troubled past.

[67]William Greider, "The Education of David Stockman," *The Atlantic*, CCXLVIII (Dec. 1981), 30.

IN EARLY 1978 Dr. Earl Ramer, a former UT professor and popular civic leader, was approached by a group of business people and public officials led by E.B. Copeland and asked to lend his name to the effort to bring metropolitan government to Knoxville and Knox County. "Given the opposition to annexation and the growing city problems," Ramer recalled later, "the idea made sense to me, and I allowed them to make me president of Citizens for Knoxville-Knox County Government." Chosen because of his widespread popularity (in 1971-1972 he had been president of the National Collegiate Athletic Association) and because of his lack of political scars, Ramer thus became involved in the movement which, along with the World's Fair, many thought would move Knoxville decisively into a new golden age.[1]

Indeed, there was considerable overlapping of support for both schemes. Local businessmen E.B. Copeland, James Dempster, and James Haslam had tried for some time to find economic and political solutions to Knoxville's dilemmas. So had UT President Edward Boling; the Greater Knoxville Chamber of Commerce; and public officials like County School Superintendent Mildred Doyle, County Judge Howard Bozeman, County Trustee Bob Broome, and Mayor Randy Tyree. All except Tyree had been intimately involved from the early stages in planning the campaign for metro government. In fact, Ramer was but the titular head of the movement, and these people formed the true nucleus.[2] Assuming that county citizens would oppose metro government, campaign strategists planned to sell the concept hard in both areas, in the city promising lower taxes and in the county raising the fears of annexation if metro government were not approved. Large community meetings were scheduled, as were talks before civic clubs, a door-to-door campaign, and heavy advertising using supporters with high name recognition.

But metro backers underestimated both their opposition and the traditional intransigence of the voters. Cas Walker immediately raised howls of

[1]Interview with Dr. Earl Ramer, Aug. 15, 1979.
[2]Ibid.

Cas Walker, 1982, aged but still combative

KNOXVILLE *News-Sentinel*

protest, once telling the mild-mannered and courtly Ramer, "I don't want to *talk* about it—I want to fight it." Walker and others turned the public meetings into loud anti-metro harangues. As opponents became more vocal, some corporate contributors to the pro-metro war chest got nervous and pulled out, leaving the Citizens for Knoxville-Knox County Government perpetually short of funds. In the end, the metro referendum carried in the city but failed to secure the necessary majority in the county.[3]

Upon reflection, even Ramer explained the defeat of metro government as an anti-Expo splashover. Such observers argued that the voters, deprived of a referendum on the Expo question, were taking out their hostility toward the Expo forces in other ways. And that explanation is a reasonable one, since many of metro government's key instigators were also strong supporters of the World's Fair. Thus, the metro government vote can be interpreted in a larger sense as expressing a typical Knoxvillian ambivalence toward change and growth. Since the Civil War this resistance had never been far from the surface, encountered anew with every wave of in-migration and every proposal to bring Knoxville a fuller share of the fruits of the New South.[4]

That this resistance reappeared, still strong, in the late 1970s is perhaps the supreme irony, for then it appeared that the promise of the New South, so long awaited, might at last actually be fulfilled. As the Northeast and Midwest staggered under high energy costs, sagging economic bases (automobile manufacturing, for example), urban blight, crime, racial hostility, and violence, the South and Southwest—with their natural beauty, comparatively newer cities, and continuing veneration of family, church, neighborhood, and social control—appeared more alluring to an increasingly confused nation. Hence, men and women whose goal had been to leave the South for the more cosmopolitan and dynamic Northeast began to reassess their ambitions, while northerners who would never have moved south before began to do so in increasing numbers. Knoxville had already benefited from these business, professional, and technological newcomers, and there were indications that the city and county would continue to do so. For example, the 1980 census revealed that Knox County was the only metropolitan county in Tennessee that had grown in population since 1970. And Expo promoters, like modern-day Henry Gradys, promised that Knoxville would be even more seductive to new business and new residents in the future.[5]

To be sure, there were doubts. True, the new business-developer bloc had

[3]Ibid.; *News-Sentinel*, Nov. 8, 1978.
[4]Interview with Ramer, Aug. 15, 1979.
[5]See preliminary report on 1980 Census, prepared by U.T. Center for Business and Economic Research, Knoxville. See also "After Expo" (a report prepared by Regional/Urban Design Assistance Team [RUDAT], Mar. 1979).

World's Fair Site as it looked in the 1920s

PHOTOGRAPH TAKEN FROM THE HILL AT THE UNIVERSITY OF TENNESSEE IN THE 1920s,
WHEN THE AREA WAS KNOWN AS "SCUFFLETOWN"
UNIVERSITY OF TENNESSEE PHOTOGRAPHIC SERVICES

triumphed, aided in part by newcomers and by bolder members of older elite groups. This triumph was underlined in December 1978 when *The South Magazine*, a publication serving southern business people, listed Knoxville's most powerful men; almost all were members of the business-developer bloc once headed by Kyle Testerman. But resistance to this group had been extremely strong; the group had lost at least as many battles as it had won, including the damaging defeat of metro government.[6]

Other doubts surfaced as well. On December 29, 1980, the *Wall Street Journal* published an article on the 1982 World's Fair strongly hinting that Jake Butcher and his clique would gain the most from the enterprise, that the scheme was enmeshed in politics, that potential exhibitors were dragging their feet, that few tourists would attend, and that the Knoxville taxpayers would be left holding the financial bag. The article, titled "What if You Gave a World's Fair and Nobody Came?" was widely publicized in Knoxville, much to the consternation of the fair's promoters and to the glee of the last-ditch opponents. Local reaction to the article demonstrated that, even as highway improvements were being made and buildings were going up on the Expo site, the community was still deeply divided over what Knoxville's future should be.[7]

In 1904, those Americans who went to the St. Louis Exposition were titillated and entertained as they gawked at Nancy Columbia, "the first native esquimeaux." Americans at the turn of the century were aware that the United States was coming of age as a great power. We celebrated our progress and maturity by peering at the recreated villages of bagobos, Negritos, and Bontoc "barbarians" and thrilled to the delectable contrast of civilization and barbarism: "Igorot braves bow to the rising Sun, kill a dog, and dance on one side of the frail bamboo stockade, while on the other side, at the same hour, the neatly uniformed scouts from the civilized tribes stand at attention as the United States flag is raised to American music." The United States of 1904 thrilled to the Igorot dog feast or the Bontoc courtship dance as a people who had conquered a continent and had risen from the frontier wilderness of the Louisiana Purchase days to an immense industrial power. The young nation was now a burgeoning colonial empire, and it had a striking new role in world affairs, which would be enshrined one year later in 1905 at the treaty-making held in Portsmouth, New Hampshire to end the Russo-Japanese War.

But those who came to Knoxville's World's Fair were different from their grandparents who visited the 1904 Exposition. Henry Grady, who died in 1889, nearly at the end of the century, would have understood the industrial

[6]*The South Magazine*, Dec. 1978.

[7]*Wall Street Journal*, Dec. 29, 1980. For local reaction see *News-Sentinel*, Dec. 30, 1980. For an article similar to that of the *Wall Street Journal*'s see *New York Times*, May 30, 1981.

The World's Fair site, with the University of Tennessee, Knoxville,
campus in the background, 1982

WITH PERMISSION OF KNOXVILLE INTERNATIONAL ENERGY EXPOSITION (KIEE)

confidence that looked upon the Bontocs as part of a "savage heritage" we had surpassed. But we, heirs of his New South industrialism, may have some second thoughts. Modernization has, in many respects, despoiled our landscapes, choked our cities, and polluted our air. We may feel, therefore, that in an age of energy crises and declining nonrenewable resources, our own technology has failed us. Thus, the energy theme of the fair is a disquieting one that reveals the shortcomings of modernization.

As we looked at the Appalachian Folklife Exhibit of the World's Fair, we looked with new eyes and chastened attitudes. We cannot view our Appalachian past as "quaint" or romantic. As we contemplate the Appalachian symbols of our fair, we should utilize our Appalachian heritage to place our modernized heritage in perspective—not gawking at "hillbillies" as our forebears gawked at the Igorots, but rather with an informed sympathy because of what we know has transpired in our city and our region. Surely no one wants to retain the past for its own sake—to keep the Appalachia that was synonymous with overworked, eroded, slashed, and burnt land, the Appalachia of despoiled strip-mined land, the Appalachia of poor education and cultural deprivation, the Appalachia that is synonymous with poverty. Granted, all that was and in some cases still is part of Appalachia, but only quixotic fools embrace unselectively the whole of a past as a model for the future or a comfort for the present.

As we enrich our understanding of where we are by contemplating the interplay of these symbols of the World's Fair in our minds, we must be cautious of overdrawing the arguments. Just as modernity brings blessings as well as curses, so Appalachia does the same. We must not escape to a stylized, idealized, Appalachia—one of imagined extreme individuality, self-sufficiency, and independence because we feel that technology has failed us—any more than we should escape to an idealized notion that technology will solve all our problems. As we look at our city's past, in its Appalachian and New South modes, we can perhaps appreciate the dangers of stereotypes and the real complexities of the past and perhaps understand that history begins where idealization ends.

But as Knoxvillians peered backward into their checkered past and forward into their uncertain future, post-World's Fair events only served to heighten the city's ambivalence toward the postindustrial age. For one thing, the World's Fair site, for all the ballyhoo, after November 1982 began to deteriorate badly. True, a site developer had been found (Fairfield Properties), but arguments with UTK, local merchants, and the city seriously threatened redevelopment. Only time will tell whether Knoxville can build on the World's Fair to aid its own downtown rejuvenation.

More seriously, in late January 1983 the banking empire of Jake Butcher and his United American banking group began to deteriorate. Butcher had been one of the chief fair promoters and financiers and (as it turned out) had loaned an enormous percentage of the UAB assets to friends and cohorts, many of whom planned to make financial killings from the World's Fair. Faced with state and FDIC audits, on January 29, 1983 Butcher stepped down as president of UAB. By mid-February frantic efforts by Butcher and other stockholders to save the bank proved to be in vain, and the bank was closed. Ultimately it was absorbed into the First Tennessee banking group.

Far more important than Butcher's rapid demise was the reaction to that news by Knoxvillians. Many of the old elite and the business-progressive bloc openly gloated over Butcher's fall. More sensible was the response of many Knoxvillians: Butcher was wrong (and possibly indictable), they believed, but his boldness had carried Knoxville into a new era. Those Knoxvillians did not want to return to the past, of hostility to change, of an enormously conservative banking community, of a city closed to outsiders and new ideas. Many believed Butcher's fall would set post-fair Knoxville back at least two decades.

One can only guess the extent to which post-fair developments will affect the city. In the past, forward and progressive surges have generally died awash in the inertia of an ambivalent citizenry. The past, however, need not be a model for the future.

AS WE BEGAN THIS WORK, one of the things which impressed us was the bountiful amount of primary material which exists on the history of Knoxville and the comparative paucity of secondary works. Betsey Beeler Creekmore's *Knoxville* (Knoxville, 3rd ed., 1976) is interesting and well-written but barely scratches the surface of the city's history. Mary U. Rothrock, ed., *The French Broad-Holston Country: A History of Knox County, Tennessee* (Knoxville, 1946) and Lucile Deaderick, ed., *Heart of the Valley: A History of Knoxville, Tennessee* (Knoxville, 1976) both are excellent starting places, although both suffer from the inevitable unevenness of multi-authorship. William J. MacArthur, Jr.'s introductory chapter in the latter is an especially good interpretive survey. But, as this essay hopes to point out, much more work is needed before we can say that the story of Knoxville's past is complete.

A wealth of primary material is housed in a number of local archives. The McClung Historical Collection of the Lawson McGhee Library contains riches that are only beginning to be tapped. Similarly, the Knoxville-Knox County Archives offer the curious and determined a bonanza of material, from voting registration records to legislative, judicial, law enforcement, school, and social data. The Metropolitan Planning Commission contains a number of sources from which one can trace the evolving city. Too, the Tennessee Valley Authority has collected an enormous amount of material pertinent to the city's history. Finally, the University of Tennessee Library houses numerous federal, state, and local documents helpful to Knoxville historians. All the above repositories have professional staffs, eager to turn from their day-to-day concerns to aid the inquisitive local historian.

As we examined these and other records, we found a wealth of untapped material and a number of gaping holes in the study of Knoxville's past. To begin with, Knoxville's black population has been insufficiently studied. Rothrock's *The French Broad-Holston Country* is very useful for other topics but woefully incomplete when surveying Knoxville's blacks. Deaderick's *Heart of the Valley* is even more lacking in this area. Charles S. Johnson's "The Negro Population of the Tennessee Valley," an exhaustive study done for TVA (1934), is an excellent place to start, but virtually no one has taken advantage of this survey. On the other hand, a few topics on Knoxville's blacks have been treated well. Sally Ripatti's "Black Political Involvement in Late Nineteenth Century Knoxville," an unpublished essay (1976) was very helpful to us and offers much food for thought to those who see Knoxville as a "model city" for blacks in the late nineteenth century. Lester Lamon's "Tennessee Race Relations and the Knoxville Riot of 1919," East Tennessee Historical Society *Publications*, 41 (1969), 67-85, is very interesting, although subsequent studies may add more to our knowledge of this incident. Merrill Proudfoot's *Diary of a Sit-In* (Chapel Hill, 1962) is excellent. Other primary and secondary studies, such as Kenneth T. Jackson, *The Ku Klux Klan in the City, 1915-1930* (New York, 1967), 59-65; Knoxville-Knox County Community Action Committee, *Poverty in Knoxville and Knox County* (Knoxville, 1973); and J. Harvey Kerns, *Social and Economic Conditions in Knoxville, Tennessee, as They Affect the Negro* (Atlanta [?], 1967) are also good starting places. Yet much work needs to be done. The Beck Cultural Exchange Center contains some untapped material (including probably the best, although still woefully incomplete, collection of black newspapers), and we urge researchers not to ignore that center of black history and culture.

Extremely useful to us and to subsequent researchers will be the plethora of public and semipublic studies of Knoxville conducted at the behest of public agencies. We especially recommend the following: William J. Durbin, "Household Equipment Survey, Knoxville, Tennessee, 1934" (TVA-CWA Project 76B, TVA Technical Library); Knoxville Housing Authority, "Real Property Inventory and Low Income Housing Area Survey" (WPA Project 665-44-3-11, 1939); Hammer and Company Associates, "The Economy of Metropolitan Knoxville" (Washington, prepared for MPC, 1962); Real Estate Research Corp., "Trends, Conditions and Forecasts of Knoxville's Economy" (prepared for MPC, 1964); various studies of industrial sites in the Metropolitan Planning Commission Industrial Sites File; Hammer and Company Associates, "Knoxville's CBD" (Atlanta, prepared for MPC, 1955); Larry Smith and Company, "Market Square Development Feasibility Study" (prepared for MPC, 1960); A.J. Gray, "Center City Major Studies and Project Proposals, 1930-1973" (prepared for Center City Task Force, 1974, copy in MPC files); MPC, "The Downtown Knoxville Story" (Knoxville, 1965); Stone and Webster Engineering Company, "Site Proposal for the New National Accelerator Laboratory" (Oak Ridge, 1965); MPC and East Tennessee Development District, *General Plan, 1990* (Knoxville, 1970); Regional/Urban Design Assistance Team [RUDAT], "After Expo" (Knoxville, 1979, MPC files). Especially recommended is the 1962 Hammer Report.

Beyond these studies, Knoxville newspapers contain an anticipated wealth of information. The Knoxville *Journal* and the Knoxville *News-Sentinel* have dominated the market for a half-century. Both, however, must be read with considerable care. Prior to 1970 (and to some extent after that), both dailies editorialized with gusto and often "slanted" the news. Neither could be considered "objective" until quite recently, and occasionally their past editorial behavior was shameful. Neighborhood newspapers, black newspapers, and Cas Walker's colorful and occasionally libelous *Watchdog* are also useful. Interesting for the burgeoning of the affluent suburbs of West Knoxville is *The West Side Story*, a weekly.

One advantage Knoxville offers its historians is that it is the home of a major research institution, The University of Tennessee, Knoxville. Graduate students at UTK have done papers, theses, and dissertations on many areas of Knoxville's past. Most useful to us have been Charles Faulkner Bryan, Jr., "The Civil War in East Tennessee: A Social, Political and Economic Study" (unpub. Ph.D. diss., UTK, 1978); Percy M. Pentecost, "A Corporate History of Knoxville, Tennessee, Before 1860" (unpub. M.A. thesis, UTK, 1946); Todd Baker, "The Politics of Innovation" (unpub. Ph.D. diss., UTK, 1968). But others abound.

This study benefited greatly from oral interviews with some of the people who participated in the city's modern history. Our notes are insufficient to detail the knowledge gleaned from Lee S. Greene, George Fritts, Earl Ramer, Leonard Rogers, Kyle Testerman, and Cas Walker. The nature of this study did not permit us to interview many others whose names would be less recognizable. But those who would understand Knoxville's past cannot ignore the men and women still living who saw the transformations wrought in this city.

As we said at the beginning of this note, much work still needs to be done, and we encourage others to join us in doing it. The embarrassing paucity of work on Knoxville's blacks has already been mentioned. Labor history, especially of those who worked in the city's mills, has been similarly ignored, as have many Knoxville neighborhoods, Knoxville women, and other local minorities. Roger Posey's M.A. thesis on prohibition in Knoxville (UTK, 1982) was completed too late for us to use. It is quite good for what it does, but the post-1907 story desperately needs to be told. Anne Robinson's unpublished study of the Irene Hasley Home for Friendless Babies, an orphanage founded in the early twentieth century (UTK, 1978) is a model of what can be done with Knoxville's social institutions. But almost no one has taken Robinson's lead. Kevin Davis's unpublished examination of Knoxville churches and the Vietnam War (UTK, 1982) is one of the few scholarly works done on religion and society in Knoxville. More are needed. Karen Thornton's unpublished "The Elite of Knoxville, Tennessee in the Age of Jackson" (UTK, 1978) is excellent, but much more ought to be done on this topic, especially after 1865. John William Routh's "The John R. Neal Law School" (unpub., UTK, 1979) studies one avenue of social mobility in the city. Again, we need more work here. Almost no practitioners of the new social history or historical demography have used Knoxville as their subject. Entrepreneurial history is almost nonexistent.

In sum, the authors hope that they have offered an interpretive history of Knoxville that is meant to encourage, not discourage, others. To all who are interested in the city's past, the challenges and opportunities are still largely before us.